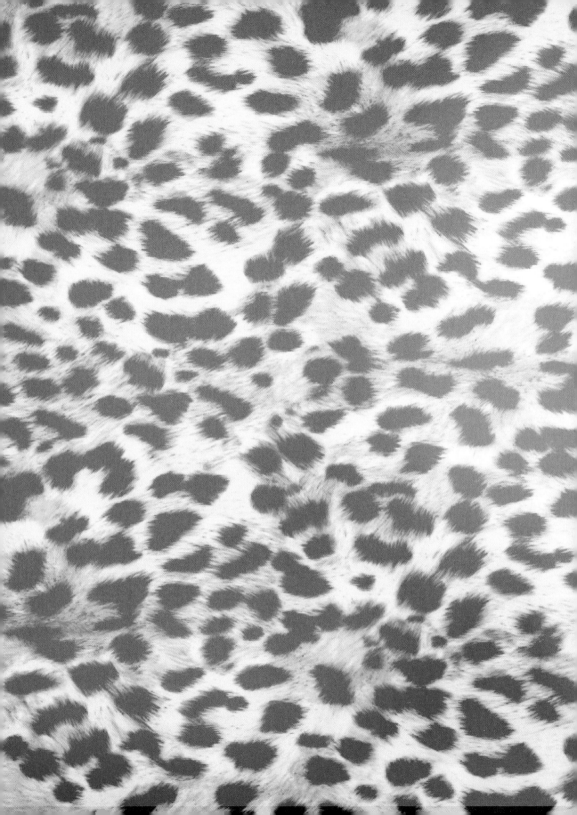

PULP ROMANCE FOR MODERN WOMEN

LOVE

PULP ROMANCE FOR MODERN WOMEN

STREET

LEAH RACHEL

MORROW GIFT
An Imprint of HarperCollins Publishers

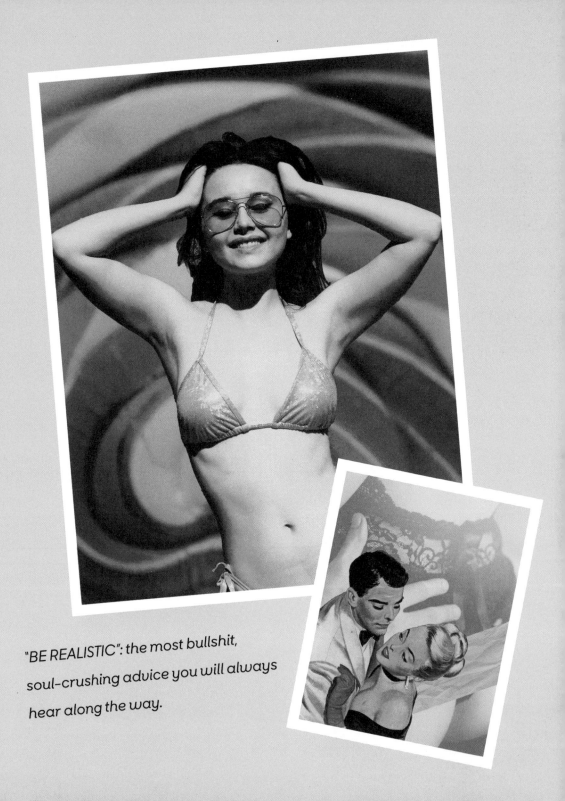

"BE REALISTIC": the most bullshit, soul-crushing advice you will always hear along the way.

For brokenhearted girls who will always love again . . .

*I want someone
who makes me
feel the way
music does.*

LOVE STREET | LEAH RACHEL

CONTENTS

Dear Readers...

To know me is to know that I have loved you. Probably too much, probably too soon, and probably too intensely. Ever since I was a little girl I've just loved...harder. Perhaps I learned too early that the things you hide in your heart will eat you the fuck alive... You see, for the better part of my life, I easily gave other people the power to love me, fix me, and make me feel "grander" than I was—I also usually gave this power to those who were unattainable or unin- terested. I battled with impulse control and would easily abandon my own life with a certain level of what-the-fuckery to chase the object of my affection. "Sport d'amour" they call it in France. It was like every new relationship allowed me to feel ALIVE. Each new love bubble gave me purpose and identity and cute stories to tell my friends about how he tickled my back as we listened to Van Morrison and kissed the world away. I was addicted to the high of falling in love and terrified of the intimacy that followed—because when things became real . . . so did the risk of abandonment. Because of this, I unknowingly fell in in lust with men I couldn't have. But you see, this "love" distracted me from my anxieties and fears about my own life and identity . . . this "love" allowed me to escape. And like all drug addicts . . . I am an escape artist.

I remember the first time I felt it. Pure, unadulterated dopamine straight to the heart, like sleeping in on a snow day when you were eleven years old. The weightless float I felt deep in my belly, as if flying high on a swing, the clamminess of my hands, the

pitter-patter in my heart . . . it took me thirty-two years to realize

that this feeling wasn't love. It was wonderful, but it wasn't love.

Love doesn't scare you, or make you feel like you're about to rob

a bank. Love cradles you and sneaks up on you and makes you

feel safe and secure and like you're alone with someone together.

Love is a best friend that you want to die with. Love is you telling

him you'll suck his dick if he can find your missing sock. (He finds

it very quickly.) Love is calm and simple and terrifying. It is nothing

that I thought and everything that I wanted.

Since starting this book, I slipped in love. Real l-o-v-e. It didn't

feel like falling, it felt like melting into molten lava together—there

were no games, there were no questions — I am still confused and overwhelmed at how simple it all really was. Either way, nobody

knows anything. Including me …

   So take what you will from the following pages, and ignore the

genders—love is love is love is love.

   And remember, no matter what the big bad humans tell you,

it's always better to be a little too much a little too soon than a little

too little a little too late …

Love always,

Leah

GEORGE

from the beach!

Trying to Figure Out
What's Wrong with Him
Before He Figures Out
What's Wrong with Me

One day we'll look back on this period of unemployment and wish we had called it FREEDOM.

W hat kind of camera is that?"

I looked up and shielded my eyes from the morning ocean mist. "It's an 8 mm. My uncle fixed it for me," I replied to this tall, dark stranger like the basic, artsy bitch I was.

It was early Tuesday morning, 6 a.m. to be exact, and I had decided to be one of those girls who loves life and wakes up to film the sunrise. It was hard to see because the wind was blowing and the tide was high. I guess ocean spray is actually a real thing and not just a cranberry juice cocktail that reminds me of bladder infections.

"I used to have one of those. They're a real pain in the ass. Make everything look really beautiful, though."

I looked up again at the stranger hovering above me, this time noticing the surfboard in his hand.

"You live around here?" I asked.

"Yeah, just around the block. Here, let me see the camera." The wind died down for a second and I blocked the sand from hitting the lens as I passed the stranger my camera. I don't know why I did it. Yes I do. Did I mention the stranger was bloody gorgeous? Dirty, hot, bearded, he was a real fucking man.

And he wanted to hold my camera! "I'm going to film you. Don't pay attention."

I immediately got weird and paid attention.

"Why?" I asked.

"Because I want you to see how beautiful you look right now."

As I awkwardly acted normal and got really weird about what to do with my hands, I let the surfing stranger film me. After about

30 seconds he passed the camera back to me, smiled, and went on his merry way. I watched him disappear down the old beach boardwalk until he was a tiny speck, and then he was no more.

Frozen in the charming stranger's wake, I took a seat on the sand with complete disregard for the camera or its fragile, sensitive lens. (I ruined it that day, btw.) *Damn,* I thought. *Now that was some* American Beauty *shit.*

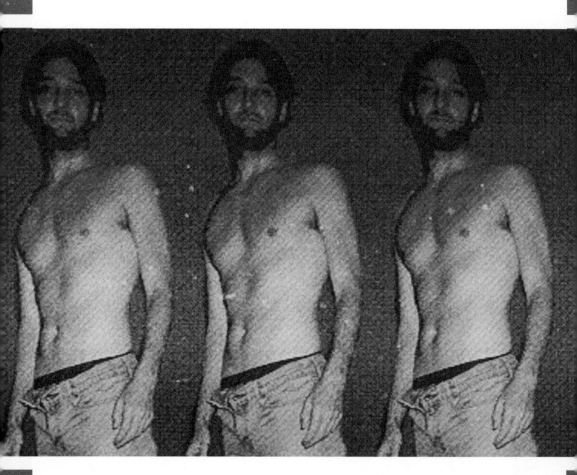

"I didn't even get his name!" I complained to my friends later that day as I shoveled a spoonful of poke into my overly lip-glossed mouth like an anxiety-ridden female version of the prince in *Cinderella*. My friends all sort of ignored me, refusing to fuel my projection fire. I guess I did sort of have a bit of a habit of romantically projecting onto strange men I met in what I considered serendipitous circumstances. (There was Ryan, who I met during jury duty, and Frankie, who I started texting after he rear-ended me—with his car.)

"If you're meant to be in each other's lives you'll run into him again, I promise," one of my friends reassured me.

"And if I don't?" I asked.

But I didn't need an answer. Because somewhere deep in my belly, beneath the poke and matcha and Sour Patch Kids and Klonopin, I KNEW THAT I WOULD.

And fail me not, my gut was right.

Just two days later, I called off work with an awful case of the fuck-its and decided to have a "me day." So there I was, lying in the middle of the beach with the rest of the superrich and/or unemployed, when whose shadow blocked the sun from reaching chapter 5 of the *The Power Within*? My stranger! My Prince Charming. My—

"George."

I acted like I just then noticed him. "Huh?"

"My name. It's George."

I smiled. "Hi, George," I said, absolutely loving the way his name sounded rolling off my tongue. (George! So timeless, so underrated, so classic.)

After some short chitchat about how weird this twice-in-three-days run-in was, I invited George to sit down with me and share my turkey sandwich. He couldn't, he said, he had to meet his buddies out at the breakwater for the afternoon surf. I briefly wondered what George did for a living that afforded him all this time to surf. He was probably really rich. Yes! A rich artist. His beard said so. Either that or some sort of famous photographer—you know, with the way he took my camera that first day and all.

Or maybe he was a bum like me? A 28-year-old college dropout who was still figuring out what she wanted to be when she grew up. Naw. He looked like success. His name was GEORGE, after all.

"Lemme get your number, though," he said before he left.

I asked for his phone, but to my surprise, he said he didn't have one. "Oh, right. Duh. You're surfing."

"No." He shook his head. "I mean I don't have one at all."

After a long pause I felt my innards rumble. "That's beautiful," I said. *Yep,* I thought, *he's DEFINITELY an artist.*

I gave George my number verbally, and he swore he'd remember it. I didn't want to risk it, so I tried to write it down on a piece of paper and give it to him—but he was already gone. *Please let him remember it,* I literally prayed to the shitting seagulls above. *Please!*

RING RING RING!

Two days later, right as I was going into a fuck-that-motherfucking-tease spiral, I got a call from an 800 number. It was George, of course, and he was calling from a pay phone. And just like that, pay phones were sexy as fuck and 1-800 numbers would forever dampen my romance-hungry panties.

BURY YOUR HEAD IN A BOOK AND IGNORE THE WORLD TODAY!

On our first date, he walked to pick me up, like a true gentleman. There was something so old-school about him. So connected to every moment and every word. Perhaps it was the no-phone thing, but George from the Beach was literally the most present human being I had ever met. And goddamn was it intoxicating.

I loved how he looked into my eyes as I told him stories. How he didn't care about status updates or mutual friends. I loved how we walked everywhere and never took his car. I loved how he paid in cash and often didn't wear shoes. I loved how he called me from random numbers and showed up at my door often without warning. I loved everything about George, and I couldn't wait for him to meet my friends.

Our third date was when things started to get a little weird. We had had some beers at a boardwalk bar, and it turned out George had forgotten his wallet. No biggie, I could pay. He ran into an old friend of his who was roller-skating by with a snake wrapped around his shoulders.

"Yo, bitch! You owe me twenty dollars!" the street performer barked at our outdoor table.

"What was that all about?" I asked George as he chugged the rest of his Blue Moon.

"Oh, that's Ricardo. He's probably high."

I laughed. I didn't know what else to say. Were they friends? Was that his drug dealer?

"Let's go back to your place," I said, instead of pressing the subject.

"Shit, we can't. Not tonight. My place is messy."

I told him I didn't care and that I loved messy. He said not this kind of messy. I felt creeped out a little by the snake charmer, and I think the beer was going to my head, so I decided to call it a night.

"Can I sleep over?" George asked as the California sky uncharacteristically started to drizzle.

"Um, sure," I said, unaware of where the night was going to take us.

He took a two-hour shower that night, and I'm pretty sure he stole one of my soaps. Not to mention 40 dollars from my wallet and a bag of Kettle chips. I somehow justified the missing stuff from my apartment to myself.

My friends were begging to meet him, so when he called me a few days later and invited me out, I said, "My friends are going out, too! Let's all hang out together!"

George liked the idea, and pretty soon all seven of my B-list friends were just as in lust with George as I was. One thought she recognized him from an American Apparel ad a few years ago, and another

swore she had run into him at a rave downtown. He was an international man of mystery. He was MY international man of mystery. But later that night, George became more than that.

The moon was full, and as George and I sat on my apartment roof in sweatpants and ate nachos, I couldn't help but feel so comfortable I started to cry. "I'm sorry," I sniffled. "It's just been a long time since I've felt so cozy around someone. It's like you don't even care about how . . . how . . ."

"How what?" he sweetly asked, completely void of prediction or judgment.

"How fucking lost I am," I wailed as I dipped back in for a handful of nachos. And then George just shut the fuck up and let me spill to him. About my lack of career. My lack of dreams. My lack of direction. He held me close that night and stroked my hair like a best friend in middle school would have as I cried myself into a salty, swollen, teary-eyed slumber.

When I woke up, George from the Beach was gone.

I felt emotionally cleansed and eager to see my cuddly beach beau again, as I rounded the corner for a hot cup of coffee and perhaps even a croissant.

AND THERE—in the alley behind the coffee shop by the beach—was George. Inside a dumpster.

"GEORGE?" I yelled.

"Hi! Good morning. Sorry, I had to start my day. Didn't mean to sneak out on you."

I continued to stare. Dumbfounded. "George, what are you doing in there?"

He didn't answer. Instead, obviously smelling like garbage, he followed me into the coffee shop and ordered a latte and three hard-boiled eggs, on me.

As he cracked open his eggs at a tiny outdoor table, I suddenly noticed the dirt beneath his fingernails.

"Protein." He smiled. "Eat enough of these and you basically don't gotta eat anything else all day!" I sipped my iced coffee and chewed on the straw, staring at my new boyfriend as some *Sixth Sense*–type shit ran rapidly through my mind. (What *was* his job? Why had I never been to his house? The missing Kettle chips, those long showers, the lack of phone…)

"George, can I ask you something? And you promise not to lie?"

"Of course," he said through a clearly never-braced smile.

"George…*are you homeless*?"

He finished off the third hard-boiled egg before answering me. "I'm not *homeless*. I just don't have a home."

I'M SORRY, WHAT?!

He did nothing wrong, I suppose. Because he didn't technically ever lie to me. I guess I just never asked.

I bid him farewell and gave him 20 bucks before walking down the long boardwalk to my apartment. And there, as I passed a sleeping bag next to a half-erected, sand-scratched tent on the beach, was a half-eaten bag of jalapeño Kettle chips.

Now, years later, I still occasionally run into George along the boardwalk. We always nod at each other and smile—me on my way to get poke, he on his way to surf. (Where *did* he get that surfboard, by the way????) Me on my way to keep trying to figure out what to do with my life, he on his way to doing nothing all day and loving it.

I dated a guy named Derrick for nine months right after George. Derrick was a fashion designer with a vintage Jaguar in his garage and a retractable ceiling in his bedroom. He didn't have a home; he had a compound. After Derrick, I dated an actor named Ryan, who lived in L.A., Sydney, and New York. He didn't have a home, either. He had three.

I wasn't in love with either, and neither made me feel safe or cozy.

I missed George. And his beach.

Born with a heart,
Enlarged from the start,
Just a matter of time,
'Til her world fell apart.

HEAD: Buy toilet paper, Epsom salts, and other things to improve your life.

HEART: Research celebrity skin-care regimens, then purchase overpriced face products that don't ever work.

HEAD: Just a trim, please.

HEART: Fuck it, cut it all off. And while you're at it, get me four lychee martinis and a telephone. Time to quit my job, buy a motorcycle, and contact a ladies' intelligence agency that can help me change my identity and start a brand-new life.

HEAD: Go to work, hustle hard, impress your boss, and be kind to your coworkers.

HEART: Quit at lunch, fuck the hot intern, drink water from the tap, and horrify your coworkers.

HEAD: Don't call him. He's been ignoring you. You're better than this.

HEART: Go ahead! Do it! Fuck up your life!

HEAD: Get your shit together, go to work, and stop feeling sorry for yourself.

HEART: Smoke some weed you find on the kitchen floor, throw up when you realize that it's dried broccoli, take a "me day" to deal with the trauma, drain your bank account, get an overpriced manicure.

HEAD: Go to your work drinks, eat a healthy dinner, and read a relaxing book.

HEART: Go to the strip club, make best friends with a coconut-scented dancer named Big Titty Tina, eat overpriced shrimp cocktail, make plans to abandon your lives together, combine your life savings to purchase a Triumph Bonneville, and call off work for the next four years due to an incurable case of the fuck-its.

I sexually identify as a romantic sponge with the emotional skin of a third-degree-burn victim.

My heart is all like,
Go ahead! Do it!
Fuck up your life!

HOW TO BE
BEAUTIFUL

Want to fall 60 percent in love and ignore our issues, then wake up ten years later with four

1. GAIN TEN POUNDS. And if anyone in your circle of friends shies away from you or starts positioning you weird when taking pictures because of your recent plumpery, cut them out. Cut them out FAST AND HARD. Cut them out like a 100-dollar-off coupon for Target you found in the Sunday *Times*.

2. CALL YOUR PARENTS. I know your dad was a little bit of an alcoholic and your mom was a little bit of a hooker, but GET OVER IT ALREADY. Any hard feelings past 30 are on you.

3. TELL STRANGERS THEY ARE COOL. Trust me, they need it. An in-person "like" can take someone's day from miserable, aimless, and "about to cut off their own hair" to contemplative, maybe hopeful, and "making an appointment at that cute spot that girl with good hair told them about that one time." Save a soldier, and a soldier will save you.

4. EAT LUNCH. I know that seems crazy. Breakfast is the kick-start-your-metabolism, eat-it-even-if-it-seems-like-it-will-make-you-gain-weight-because-you-don't-even-want-it-but-the-magazine-said-so meal, RIGHT? Well yeah, maybe. But something tells me that girls who eat lunch are the same girls who get what they want in bed and also tell their friends when they're acting shady. Girls who eat lunch are girls who don't hold out for shit. And whatever you do, don't order the kale Caesar or you will have completely negated the point.

5. CRY. Often. And do it whenever the fuck you want. I don't know when not crying became cool, but I do not subscribe. Emotions make people uncomfortable, but every time a woman publicly floods, she makes it okay for another girl to burst. And I think we

can all agree that most of us (especially midday on Wednesdays) are usually scratching and itching and dying to burst. Be brave. Cry, baby.

6. **FORGET ABOUT THE PLOT.** Don't spend your whole life trying to "do things." Spend it trying to be things. Being busy doesn't equal going to heaven. Also, NEWSFLASH: The moment you die is just like remembering an old movie. You don't remember jobs and story lines; you remember characters and emotions. You basically forget everything about everything—you only remember how it made you feel. (I know this not because I've died and been reincarnated but because I did a lot of peyote with my fake-hippie ex

and drank way more than I was supposed to to help me escape my crippling reality at the time.)

7. **WEAR YOUR HEART ON YOUR SLEEVE NO MATTER HOW MANY TIMES SAID SLEEVE GETS BURNED / TORN / RUINED IN THE WASHER.** The only way to prevent your heart from being broken is to act like you don't have one. Do not do this. Roll up your heart-covered sleeves and get fucking dirty. There is nothing more beautiful than a woman who has let herself love.

8. **LOVE HARD.** And give that shit away like a stranger with candy. Give it away generously to everyone who needs it or wants it or never got enough of it.

9. **TELL PEOPLE WHAT THEY MEAN TO YOU.** Tell them all the time. All the time. All the time . . .

10. **RUN THROUGH RIVERS NAKED.** Let your titties flop and fly and splash that holy water all around you. River water is far more healing than pressed juices, I assure you. And nothing feels better against naked boobies than a cool, crisp forest river.

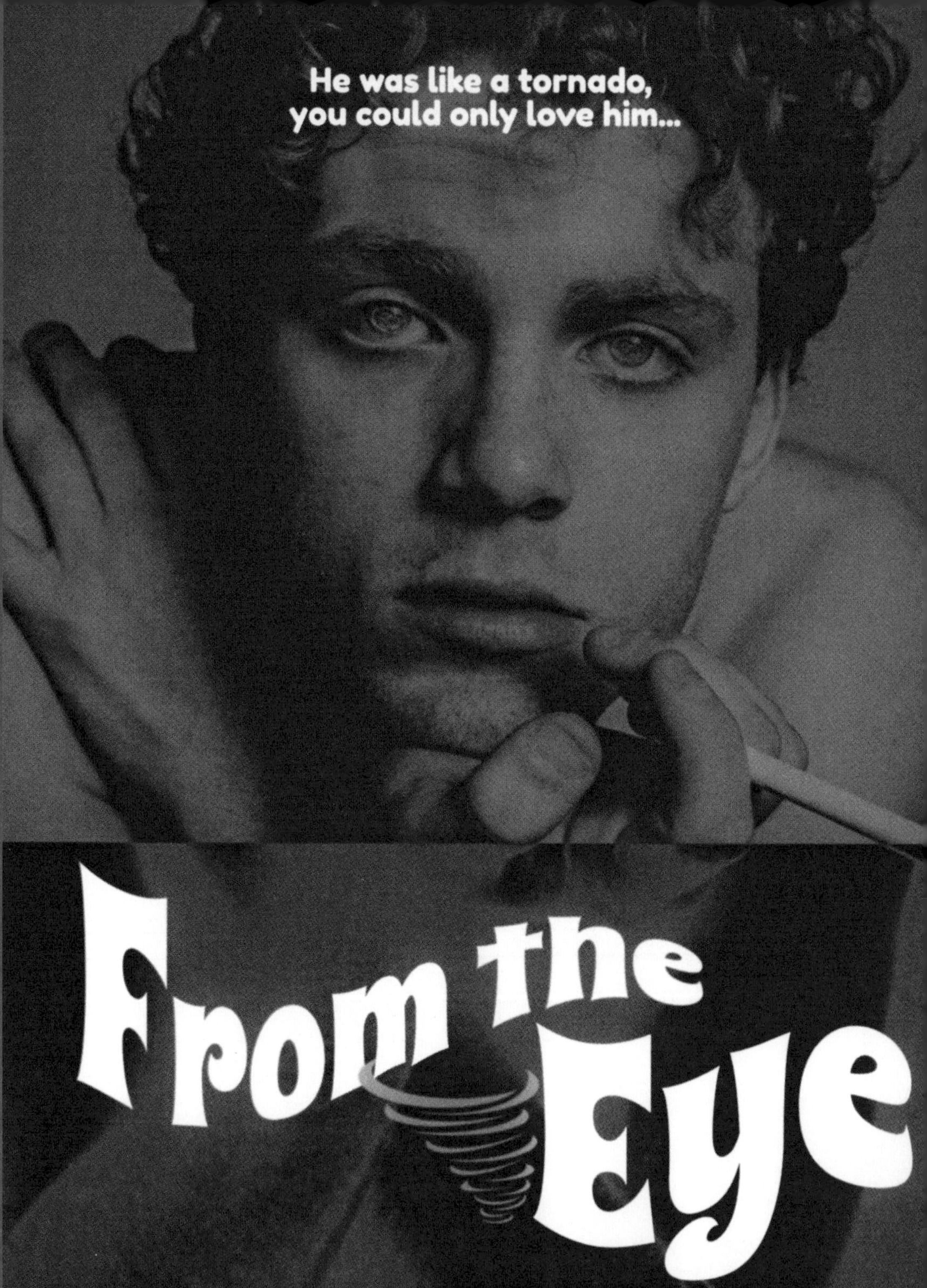
He was like a tornado,
you could only love him...
From the Eye

my ORGASM timeline
A Winding Road to Climax . . .

1990: A Little Tikes power tool. It was a battery-operated fake drill that didn't really do anything but vibrate. I took it out of my brother's toy box and pretended to want to play with it instead of my ratty-haired Barbies or Easy-Bake Oven. Barbies and ovens didn't do the trick like this go-go power tool. I held it outside my panties and sat cross-legged on my cold basement floor. I think I was five. I had accidentally brushed it across my lady garden a few weeks before and remember feeling internally electrocuted down yonder . . . in a good way. Anyway, I couldn't tell anyone else what I had discovered. I watched enough TV shows to know that if you have super-powers, you must keep them to yourself—for if you tell everyone, you risk them being taken away. I pressed the on button and moved the plastic drill down south. It was the first time I realized my pussy had power. I didn't come. I'm not even sure you *can* come at that age, but I will always get sort of horny for the rest of my life anytime I go into a Home Depot.

1993: "Let's play tornado!" I said, like I did every time Tommy came over after school. Tornado: a game where I and my 9-year-old play date huddled up in the corner of the basement on a futon and humped the living daylights out of each other while acting like we were protecting each other from an incoming tornado.

1994: A shoulder ride on a bumpy road. My Japanese uncle Oji let me sit on his shoulders as we walked down a brick road with my broth-

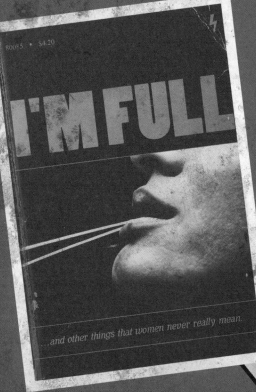

BUY BOOKS,
NOT TAMPONS.

S0085 • $4.20

I'M FULL

...and other things that women never really mean.

Name _____

Street Address _____

City/State/Zip _____

ers toward the grocery store. It had been stormy that summer, and the rain caused the bricks to shift and clutter. About halfway down the street, I held tight to Oji's salt-and-pepper hair, and with my head in the clouds, I was brought to my first official orgasm. Up until that point it had just felt good to have vibrations in that area, but this time, and God bless that old brick road . . . I finished. Completely unaware of what was happening above, Oji looked up from below as I audibly gasped. "You okay?" he asked. "Want to get down?" "I'm okay." I smiled. "Are we almost there yet?" As we approached the grocery store and my brothers and I chose TV dinners for the night with Oji, I stood a little taller than ever before. But never too tall for another shoulder ride.

1995-2000: Lots of masturbating to sexy R & B videos in my parents' room with the door locked. One explorative sleepover with two girls sometime in middle school where we grabbed each other's recently sprouted titties and I think I humped a pillow in another room until I came.

2000-2004: Sex and no orgasms. What the fuck? Penetration sucks! Especially when you're the other woman in high school and the boy you lost your virginity to is nicknamed Baby Carrot and now you know why. But on the bright side, it didn't even hurt! Other than that, it was a bunch of getting fingered by 16-year-old boy-hand jackhammers and having drunk sex with boys who were as clueless as I was. I lied and told everyone I came sooooooo many times every time. I had never come from dick yet, though. What was wrong with me? Was my

THE LATEST FROM THE EDITORS OF STEAMY RIDGES PRESS

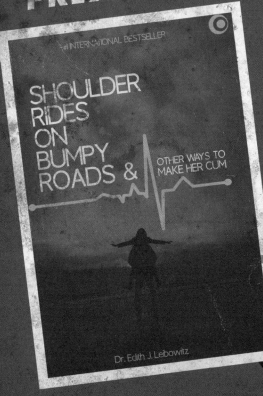

#1 INTERNATIONAL BESTSELLER

SHOULDER RIDES ON BUMPY ROADS & OTHER WAYS TO MAKE HER CUM

Dr. Edith J. Leibowitz

A Tiny Poem

"I do," she lied.

vagina broken? Was it because I masturbated too much? Too early? Why did all the *Cosmopolitan* articles make it seem so easy? Why didn't dick work?!

2006: The first man-made orgasm I had as a grown human girl was given by the drummer of a band named Snow Nose. At the time, I was so naive and corn-fed I literally didn't know what "snow nose" meant. Did he enjoy baking? Soothing his chafed nose with talcum powder? Whatever. Who cares? He was Australian, and he was in a band. I met him lying in the glass box at the Standard hotel on the Sunset Strip of Los Angeles, California. Yeah, that's right. MY JOB WAS LYING IN A GLASS BOX. I wasn't naked; I was to wear "girly pajamas," preferably all pink or all white. I couldn't drink a lot of water during the day, prior to my shift, because the shifts were four hours, and I couldn't get out to pee. So obviously my career was going well and my life was full of promise. But I couldn't make my parents too proud, ya know. So one night, after my 8 p.m. to 12 a.m. shift, I sat at the nearby bar (still in my white pajamas) and ate my employee meal next to a group of gorgeous, eyeliner-wearing, leather-jacket-donning bad boys I had seen come in and out of the hotel earlier. They told me the name of their band, and I pretended to LOVE their music. I didn't want to go home yet, because at the time, I shared a one-bedroom apartment with a stripper named Candy, and as of late, she had been inviting our 50-year-old neighbor over for sleepovers in her twin bed, eight feet away from mine. So when the drummer of the band asked if I wanted to come up to his room and chill, I eagerly shoveled down the rest of my hamburger and said yes. His room was modern and angular, and by the look of the clothes draping the giant suitcase in the corner, there might be a lady involved in his life. He promised there wasn't; he just sometimes liked to dress in lady clothes. For whatever reason, the thought of this wild and free, cross-dressing Australian drummer seriously turned me on. He wasn't even trying to touch me, either, a true gentleman. We drank some fancy-ass bottled water (I was SO thirsty from dehydrating myself all day in preparation for *le box*) and smoked Camel Lights on his patio for a few hours until I got super tired and asked if I could crash there. I *was* already in my pajamas, after all! He said yes, and we cuddled as intimately as two basic strangers could cuddle. It was intimate and scary and weird and one of the situations you only get yourself into when you're 21 years old and unafraid of anything. In the morning, I turned to him and kissed him. It was morning and I was horny, and I knew I would never see him again. I grabbed his hand and put it right in the spot that worked. Note to ladies: DRUMMERS ARE GOOD WITH THEIR HANDS. As I laid back and closed my eyes, the title drummer boy pa-rum-pa-pum-pummed away and I came my brains out. If I had any brains back then, that is. I mean, I did sleep in a basic stranger's bed and put myself in "harm's way." But Drummer Boy was sweet and cool and didn't even try to fuck me. In fact, when I later tried to go down south on him, he said I didn't have to. He had a meeting to get to anyway. Electrocuted back to life, I chugged another fancy bottle of water, pressed the lobby button for the desperately modern elevator, and skipped past the empty glass box above the receptionist. After that day, I never went back to lie in the glass box again. There was too much water to drink and too many orgasms to be had. I thank Little Drummer Boy for reminding me of that.

2008: Dick finally worked! And I dated the guy for almost a year just because his penis convinced me that I was normal. And whoa, baby. It was different than the "from the outside" sensation. It was intense and powerful and wild and out of control. When I broke up with Dickmaster, I immediately bought a giant dildo from the Hustler store on Hollywood Boulevard. I needed to figure out how this thing worked. And I finally did.

2009-2015: Lots of bad boyfriends. Lots of one-night stands. About 50 percent success rate for internal OGs. Usually only when I felt comfortable enough to show them how. Usually when they grabbed my waist. Usually when they fucked me from behind.

2017: New Year's Eve. I had been dating TJ for less than a year. There was a supermoon that night and I was in super love. Maybe that's how it works after all, when you're in super love you have super orgasms? TJ was sweet and dirty and cuddly and wild all at the same time. He loved my big ass and made me feel beautiful in positions I had previously felt not. We ditched our New Year's Eve plans, because I hated New Year's Eve, and instead stayed in and cooked huge steaks sprinkled with nothing but salt. He went down on me during the countdown and I screamed as the cheering noises of neighbors echoed in the night. It was the best orgasm I've ever had. It was the holy grail. It was hilarious and ironic and erotic and amazing. I don't hate New Year's Eve anymore.

TO-DON'T LIST

Don't cry because it's over. Cry because you're a delusional mess and "it's over" *never* means it's over.

- **DON'T** order sautéed vegetables instead of fries and then spend the next four hours living in regret and later binge eat ice cream to make up for it and consume so many calories you could have just ordered four orders of fries in the first place.

- **DON'T** agree to get coffee and "catch up" with your ex (the one who proposed to you at a Thanksgiving dinner with 30 people while rolling on ecstasy).

- **DON'T** believe him when he tells you he's too busy. Nobody is ever busier than a guy who doesn't want to date you.

- **DON'T** underestimate the power of having crushes from the shadows. He doesn't not like you if he doesn't know you exist.

- **DON'T** date a guy who skips over the pistachios that are hard to open.

- **DON'T** cry because it's over. Cry because you're a delusional mess and "it's over" *never* means it's over.

- **DON'T** try to figure out what's wrong with someone before they figure out what's wrong with you.

- **DON'T** shave your fur bikini if it makes you feel warm and cuddly.

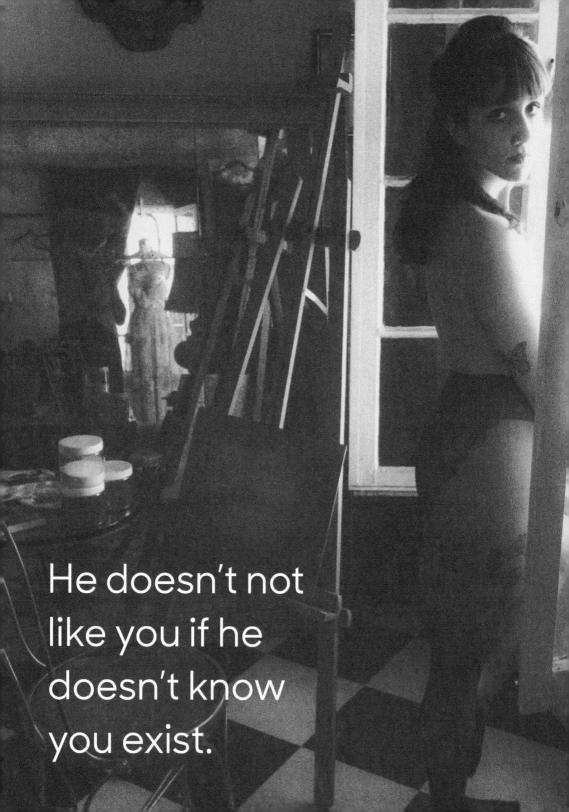

He doesn't not
like you if he
doesn't know
you exist.

- **DON'T** be ashamed to cry. Humans are the only mammals that have the ability to shed tears. It is our *Homo sapiens* superpower. (I mean, do camels spend the weekend ashamed that they spit four times this week? Do turtles get embarrassed about how much they go in and out of their shells? Hell no!)

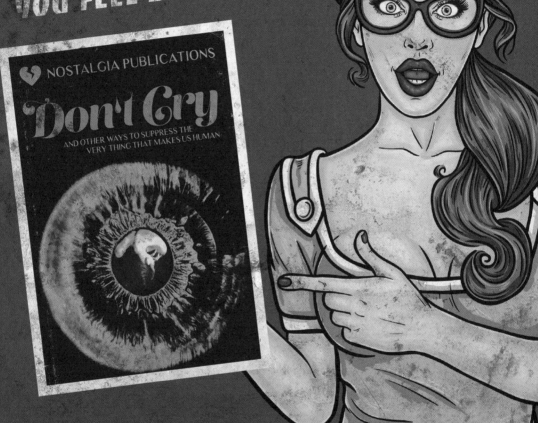

IF YOUR BAD DAY JUST GOT WORSE, BUY THIS BOOK. IT WILL MAKE YOU FEEL BETTER.

NOSTALGIA PUBLICATIONS

Don't Cry

AND OTHER WAYS TO SUPPRESS THE VERY THING THAT MAKES US HUMAN

Name _____

Street Address _____

City/State/Zip _____

CONVOS

HE JUST CAN'T WIN

"You look like a baby in that pic!"

(So what, bitch, I look old now?)

"You look so healthy!"

(So you're saying I'm fat.)

"Did you start your period?"

(Why? Because I need to be bleeding to justify having feelings?)

"I'm so full. You seriously want dessert?"

(Yes. I was not, in fact, joking about desiring something more. I know, right? What a monster! Now order me that goddamn chocolate soufflé so I can shove it down my throat and then fake a trip to the bathroom, call an Uber, and never see your "I'm so full" ass again.)

"Babe. You already told me that story. Remember?"

(Don't ever look at me like I'm a dumb forgetful bitch and you're a smart rememberful man, or I will bite your arm like I did last night, but this time I'll break skin.)

"You know who you sort of look like? A hotter Ricki Lake!"

(...)

"I do think I'm falling in love with you. I just want to be sure before I really say it."

(If it's not a "fuck yes," it's a "fuck no." Can you draw me a lukewarm bath before bed tonight so I can drown in it with you?)

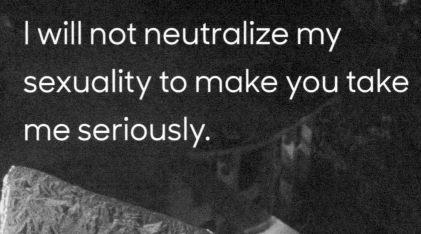

I will not neutralize my sexuality to make you take me seriously.

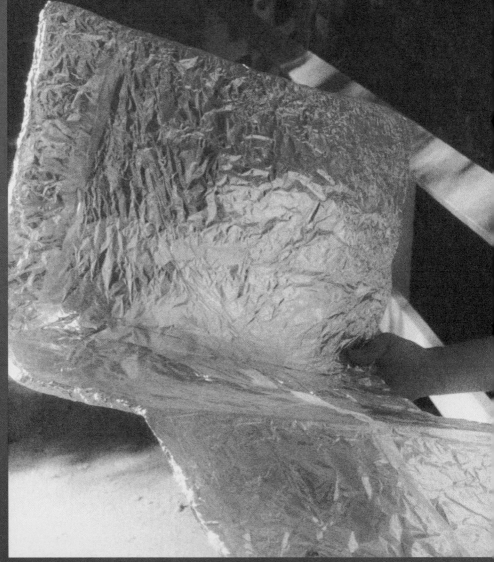

Hell hath no fury
like a woman
about to chop off
all of her hair...

LETTERS I NEVER SENT

BECAUSE WHY
LICK THE STAMP
WHEN YOU CAN
LICK A LOLLIPOP

Dear Uber Driver,

You didn't know, but my eyes weren't red and puffy because I just watched Lion; my eyes were red and puffy because my best friend just broke up with me. I think maybe you knew something else was going on, but you never asked. You only asked about the movie, in what I now realize was an effort to calm me down, and when I proceeded to completely lie and make up the entire plot (in detail, for 15 minutes) you never called me out. You said you loved the movie, too, and saw it in the theater with your son, and I was confused but happy to talk about anything other than the friendship I had just lost, and so I went full speed into "OMG and that one part with the little kid and the lion…" You had little bottles of water in your car, and you didn't bat an eye when I drank two. (Tears can be severely dehydrating, you know.) When we got close to my apartment you asked if I minded if we pulled through In-N-Out. The drive-through line was finally short and you'd been waiting for it to go down all night. I said yes and you turned off the meter and you bought me a milkshake to say thanks. I sipped the milkshake with shaky hands and wanted nothing more than to stay in the back seat of your too-warm, vanilla-scented Honda Accord all night.

On the rest of the way back to my apartment, we talked about our parents and God and how we both loved going to Niagara Falls when we were little even though everybody else hated it. We talked about that crazy lady who threw herself over the waterfall in a wooden barrel with her cat way back in the 1900s, and how crazy it is that we both looked that shit up over and over via Google spirals, well into our adulthood. I laughed and

She
remembered
her old self . . .
and then
everything
fucking
changed.

finished my strawberry milkshake, and you told me I was weird and funny and you bet I have a lot of friends. I told you not that many actually, and you looked like you didn't believe me. I told you it was true and that it was my fault because actually I can be super overbearing and selfish and suddenly disappear when a new guy enters my life, but again, you looked like you didn't believe me. My eyes started to re-well up and I quickly exited your car and never saw you again. But I wanted to make you proud. I wanted you to be right about me. I called my friend that night and she didn't pick up. I had more to say, I said. Two weeks later, after a lengthy apology about my past shiftiness, we curled up together, ordered Chinese food, and watched Lion. It was then that I realized there is no lion in Lion. Thank you, Mr. Uber Driver, for thinking I was, in fact, a good friend, and thank you, Mr. Uber Driver, for not correcting me about the stupid lion.

Dear 8-Year-Old Me,

Goddamn, girl. I wish I could be more like you. You eat whatever you want whenever you want, you literally chase boys around all day without giving a fuck, you dress up and play Queen of the

World with your best friends, you cry when you need to, and you don't care who hears you take a shit. The world will try to change you as you get older. It will tell you to hold in your crushes and your farts. It will tell you to put up walls to protect yourself, and it will tell you that to play Queen of the World you need to be tripping on mushrooms or locked up in a padded room. In many ways, you are the coolest, purest, most confident woman you will ever be in your whole entire life, and this will make no sense at all because you are only 8 years old. But I miss you all the time. Want to come over and play?

Dear Psycho Next Door:

I told all my friends about you the moment I met you. Hell, I told cashiers at Target and strangers on the street about you. I told anyone who would listen. Because holy fucking fuck nuggets, I was in love. I remember when you first moved into the apartment next door, I knocked on our shared wall and you knocked back twice. We went out into the hall to "meet our new neighbors," and less than 40 seconds after, I knew I was completely fucked. I collapsed onto my couch and told my roommate how I swore to

We were such good little girls . . . and then we quit our jobs, faked our own deaths, moved to a fuck-it cult in Canada, and lived our best lives.

God I'd met you before. Another life? A dream? Who knows? Who cares? You had a girlfriend for the first few months, so I patiently waited to cross the line. I should have respected your healing days and not invited you over for two bottles of wine and home-cooked lasagna, but I couldn't wait a second longer. After we fucked a few times you told me you weren't ready for another relationship right away. I got angry and knocked on your wall too hard and you freaked out and switched to another apartment two floors down. "What a psycho!" I told everyone. I'm sorry for misrepresenting you to a group of people you will never know. I'm sorry for making you take that shitty downstairs apartment with no balcony. I'm sorry for being a bad neighbor. I never told anyone about my banging on your wall, I never told anyone about my midnight text marathons, and I never told anyone how I accidentally, totally, and completely pushed you away. I never told them that I was, in fact, the psycho next door.

Dear Child That Never Was:

    I never thought about having one of you. Ever. Not a boy. Not a girl. Not a baby. And I'm not totally sure why. My hearty hips and tits were definitely made for it. (Except in 2005, when I had a borderline eating disorder due to anxiety attacks, frozen yogurt, and getting compliments from strangers about how good—unwomanly?—I looked.) Hip size and mental state aside, I always felt guilty for not ogling over the contents of passing strollers or letting the swollen-bellied woman at the DMV go in front of me in line. And yada yada, yackety shmackety, I know—what a monster I was. Everyone saw cute little chubby thighs and angel faces, while I saw Caucasian sausage aliens and wrinkly miniature old men. I didn't have baby fever—I had baby hypothermia. But then something happened. I met someone. And my body completely fucking turned on me.

I didn't know if it had to do with my new man's errrr . . . mature age, but around him my ovaries were snorting cocaine. Dormant for years, my feline innards were READY TO FUCKING PARTY. Let's just call the awakener of said dormant organs Mr. Man, shall we? Mr. Man was divorced and had two kids already, and until meeting him, I never realized how turned on I got around J.Crew sweaters and "Daddy days." On days when he could sneak away from the kids we would go on our own childlike dates to match. To the putt-putt course, to the diner for milkshakes, we even went to an old movie theater to watch vintage cartoons! (I know, I just choked on my own puke, too.) Mr. Man could never sleep over because he had to sleep close to his kids. At his own house. Around the block from his ex-wife. (How mature that they were making it work!) I understood his need to be close to his beloved infant spawns. My friends said my sudden baby fever had nothing to do with Mr. Man but rather with my turning 30. That it's a chemical change that happens during peak fertility years. That it was my feline side emerging. That my tits probably were in on it, too. I told them I am not an animal; I am a woman with her own wants and feelings! I am not an animal; I am a spirit! I am a fucking snowflake spirit!

Mr. Man treated me well and made me feel safe, protected, adventurous, and mature. My hips screamed for him at the end of my long waitressing shifts, and every time he came on my stomach, I couldn't help but frown at all the missed opportunities dripping and dying down my midriff, as Mr. Man swiped my skin dry with a nearby baby wipe. I figured a baby was JUST what I needed to turn my life around. It would require me to care about something more than myself and force me to stop smoking and drinking for nine whole months! A baby would make my mother happy, and a baby would give me something to plug all my unsung dreams into. Believing in myself had been hard lately, and the thought of believing in someone else instead felt like a goddamn relief. I wasn't taking birth control pills because they made me crazy, and I didn't have an IUD anymore because, no matter if it was all in my head, I SWEAR I COULD ALWAYS FEEL IT. (Fuck "The Princess and the Pea"—I was the princess and the IUD.) So there I was, little future baby, fertile as fuck and ready to procreate! I didn't tell this to Mr. Man yet, of course. He was finally breathing after his first divorce, and we'd only been dating for four months. But I thought about it all the time. I hoped he dribbled before he shot, but this man was a straight shooter from the 3-point line. No fouls. No traveling. No mistakes.

At least that's what I thought.

I was on a plane to San Francisco when I spit out my lukewarm Jack and Coke and stared out my window like Mrs. McCallister in Home Alone. *I was pregnant. I knew it.*

When I landed at SFO, I immediately turned on my phone to find five missed calls from an unknown number and one voice-mail. This was probably Mr. Man calling me from his work line to tell me he "just knew it," too. If I could feel it, he could feel it, right? I mean, this was some spiritual shit!

But me and my maybe +1 sank when we heard the voice-mail. It wasn't from Mr. Man; it was from Mr. Man's wife. She was kind and quick and was just letting me know that she existed. Her husband was a liar and this wasn't the first time it had hap-pened, and from one woman to another—"just be smarter than me and run."

I took a cab to the nearest CVS and swallowed a 40-dollar Tic Tac, chased down by a Diet Peach Snapple.

I'm not sure if you were ever really there or what you may have looked like, if you looked like anything at all. I don't know if you were a boy or a girl or just a blob of cells dealing with binary gen-der issues before making the first important choice of your life.

I didn't swallow the Tic Tac because of the revelation about Mr. Man. I swallowed the Tic Tac because of the revelation about me.

I couldn't be your mommy yet. Not because you wouldn't have had an honest father but because you wouldn't have had an honest mother. I wanted you not because I wanted to love and take care of you. I wanted you because I was sick of loving and taking care of me.

So thank you, baby / cell structure / glob that never was. You will be again someday, I think. Probably later rather than sooner, and maybe raised by me and a friend, but you will be here when I am really ready. When my mind catches up with my body.

When my spirit catches up with my animal.

Dear Disney Villains:

Jafar, Captain Hook, Scar, fuck you all. You charming, cheating, lying, riveting assholes who I'd always rather fuck than the good guy. You ruined me at five years old and you ruined me at 30. You captivating, evil, exciting little shits. I will always love you more than the prince.

Surround yourself with people who feel like starry nights and crispy fries.

THE BLIND LEADING THE BLIND

knew things were going to get weird when he showed up at my door carrying a six-pack of Red Bull Sugarfree and a _____ [NOUN]. I mean, I had always been into _____ [GENDER, PLURAL] who were a little _____ [ADJECTIVE], but this was intense, even for me. Hell, I guess that's what you get for letting the tiny, old owner of _____ [BUSINESS] set you up on blind dates. This was suitor number 3. The first date was with a polyamorous Italian prince with four _____ [ANIMAL, PLU-RAL]. He had a huge _____ [NOUN], so I went out with him again, but on date number 3 he tried to get me to have sex with him and his _____ [NOUN]. I loved the idea of polyamory, but it's hard enough for me to like one person, let alone _____ [NUMBER] or _____ [NUMBER]! Anyway, blind date number 2 was with a dude named _____ [NAME OF AN EX]. But I guess you couldn't REALLY technically call it blind, because I had met him before! Okay, dated him before. Okay, fucked him before. He was totally cool until he started yelling out "_____ [KITCHEN APPLIANCE]!" every time he came. Anyhow, for our not-blind blind date three years later, we went to eat at _____ [NAME OF RESTAU-

Sometimes ... the only thing that can get me to run two miles is listening to a contradicting podcast where my ex-boyfriend is interviewed and sounds like an idiot.

I wish I was full of donuts
instead of anxiety.

RANT]. He was rude to the waiter, told me a story about his "art" and new interest in becoming a _____ [FAKE PROFESSION], and didn't want to order any dessert. PASS. Fool me once, joke's on you. Fool me twice, joke's on me. Byyyyyyye, boy.

Okay, so back to _____ [TEMPERATURE ADJECTIVE] Red Bull guy. I thought maybe he would be lucky blind date number 3, so I tried to keep an open mind as he stood there looking _____ [ADJECTIVE] as shit in his _____ [LAME CLOTHING BRAND] jacket. I pulled out some _____ [BEVERAGE] and we both started to loosen up after our _____ [ORDINAL NUMBER] drink. He asked me how many people I had slept with, and I told him the truth: _____ [NUMBER]. He said he had only slept with _____ [NUMBER], and for some reason I found that concerning. And HERE is when the date got REALLY interesting.

"_____ [VERB]!" he suddenly exclaimed. Shit! How embarrassing. A MOUSE.

I had called the plumber last week, because I guess I thought that plumbers were exterminators. Anyway, the plumber was _____ [ADJECTIVE] enough and stayed to fix my shower drain instead.

"Do you take baths or showers more?" the plumber _____ [ADVERB] asked.

"Showers," I said.

"Funny, you look more like a bath girl."

"What the _____ [BAD WORD] is that supposed to mean?" I asked, offended.

"That you're a girl who likes to treat herself," the plumber said, and he pulled the _____ [NOUN] out of the drain.

THINGS WONDERFUL:

Talk of God, alien sex, recurring dreams

Strawberries

Big dogs

Sex at dawn

Fries with mayonnaise

Cheap sunglasses

THINGS TERRIBLE:

Talk of weather, how time flies, the housing market

Kale Caesars

Dress codes

Tapas

Catching up

"Oh, I like to treat myself, huh? Why don't you just come out and call me fat?"

Confused, the plumber quickly packed his things and left. I rolled my eyes as I saw the slogan on his pickup truck: "_____ _____ [SLOGAN]." What an asshole. He never got rid of the mouse, and also he called me fat. Treat myself! Pshh!

Oh, so back to Red Bull guy and the rodent in my apartment. I played it off like it was my pet, _____ [LITTLE GIRL'S NAME], who I had lost weeks before, and I even mustered up some tears to prove my lie. Red Bull guy bought it and scooped up the little mouse in an empty coffee can. When he asked me where its _____ [NOUN] was, I said I had thrown it out. So Red Bull guy took out a sauce pot from my cupboard and gently dropped the mousy in.

"_____ [EXCLAMATION]!" he screamed. "It bit me!"

I quickly covered the pot with a glass lid, took another shot of _____ [BEVERAGE], and rushed to get a towel. While the mouse tapped on the lid of the pot, I wrapped Red Bull guy's bleeding finger in my face towel.

"It's never bitten anyone before!" I said.

"Forget it." He stood up, grabbed a copy of _____ _____ [EMBARRASSING MOVIE YOU LIKE] sitting on my coffee table, and suggested we just watch a movie.

We never saw each other again after that _____ [ADJECTIVE] night, but two weeks later he called to tell me he had rabies.

"But we didn't even _____ [VERB]!" I exclaimed. "All we did was kiss!"

"From your fucking mouse, dipshit. It's not an STD."

"Are you going to be okay? Is there a cure? Can't you just take some _____ [MENTAL-HEALTH MEDICATION]?"

"I'm going to be fine. I just wanted you to know your pet is toxic. Goodbye."

As I hung up the phone I looked at the little mouse in the pot and said a prayer: "_____

_____ [PRAYER]." A few minutes later I gave it its last piece of _____ [ADJECTIVE] Gouda and set it free outside.

That little old shop owner never sets me up on blind dates anymore. And last time I went into her restaurant with a guy I actually met on my own and liked, she stared straight through me with her little _____ [COUNTRY ADJECTIVE] accent and told the server, "We no serve that girl with rabies."

Thanks a lot, _____ [ADJECTIVE] world. Thanks a lot.

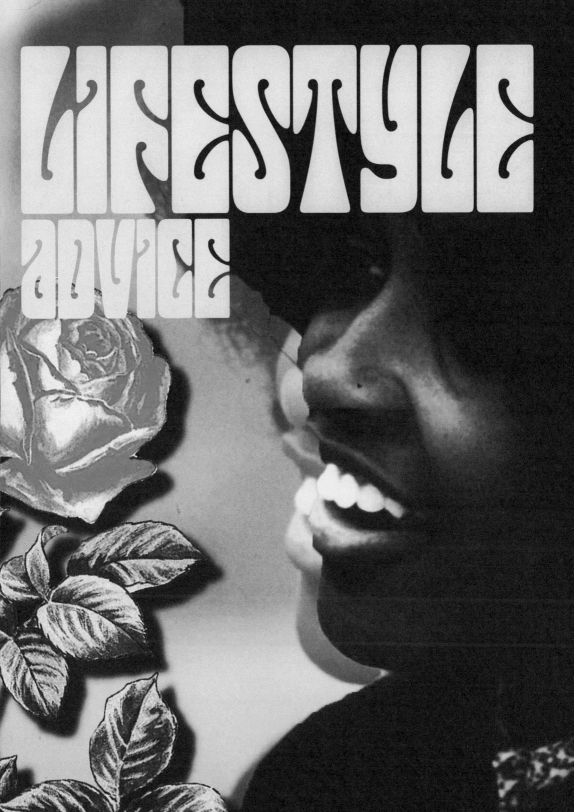

LIFESTYLE ADVICE

Iris was a thrill-seeker with eyes as blue as the sea. But you know what they say about girls named after flowers . . .

ON DIETS: Diets are for sad girls who get neutral manicures and don't contest parking tickets. Follow these simple rules and you will be happy and forever free: Drink only water and wine. If you binge eat one night, eat sushi the next. Always take cake when it's offered. And remember that artificial sweeteners kill small animals.

ON DRUGS: Never buy your own. Also, don't do cocaine when you're feeling unsure of your career choice. Always do ecstasy in the presence of bonsai trees and music. Get high while bathing once or twice. And under no circumstances ever do any form of psychedelic on a cruise ship.

ON SEX: Fuck on the first date if you want to, wait until the tenth if you so prefer. Throw away the rules, make your own, and then break those, too. Do it in daylight and try it in a park. And if you're not really looking like a possessed person with contorted eyes who's just lost feeling in the left side of their body, THEN STOP FAKING IT.

ON DATING: Do it when it's fun. Stop it when it's not. Always drink two glasses of wine before your first date and show up in a sweat-soaked maxi dress just to find out if he's really a keeper. He should love you all ways. And plus, you can only go uphill from there!

ON MONEY: You have to spend money to make money. Don't care about it and it will care about you. And no matter how rich you get, don't think you'll ever shake the poor off you. Because all the money in the world won't be able to stop you from secretly feeling like Tai from *Clueless* or getting a massive rush of dopamine straight to the heart when you hear that there's a buffet or open bar.

ON BOOBS: You remember taping them down with giant-wound-size Band-Aids, suffocating them with double sports bras, and always wearing baggy T-shirts when you slept over at your friend-with-the-sort-of-creepy-dad's house. When you were 16 a man barked at you from a pickup truck (like really, like a dog) and circled around the block again, this time with a friend. When you got that first job at 22 everyone said the only reason you got hired was because the boss just wanted to fuck you, and when you went to buy new grown-up clothes for said job, nothing ever fit quite right. Years passed, you grew up and grew out, and fell in and out of love, and fucked and got fucked, and met a man who loved your ninnies and your mind, and you realized you are sort of pretty, even beautiful, and that your boobs are your power and yours alone and they don't say anything you don't want them to say,

and that you cannot control what people hear, but you are a goddess and these are your magic girl pillows and you're going to start showing them off because you're done feeling ashamed of the very things that make you a woman.

ON LOVE: It's like God or chronic pain. You don't believe in it until you feel it. You know you're in love when you think even their ears are cute. When settling down no longer seems lame, it sort of feels more like moving into a socially acceptable heroin den with your best friend and your favorite vibrator all in one.

HOW TO CRASH IN LOVE

My manic, unreliable anxiety finds peace in your slow, brooding depression.

STEP 1: Accidentally fall in love.

STEP 2: Try to convince yourself it isn't real.

STEP 3: Brush up against them and almost get electrocuted.

STEP 4: Debate your options.

STEP 5: Realize your options are there are no options.

STEP 6: Say how you feel in some weird subliminal way and over-analyze the dilation of their pupils.

STEP 7: Notice that their pupils are fucking huge and order three more beers.

STEP 8: Completely lose it, offer your heart on a platter, and throw your dignity at the wall like a fucking dart.

STEP 9: Know that this will be the beginning of everything or the end of nothing and there's only one way to find out.

STEP 10: Dance like a fool and see if they're watching.

WHATEVER!
DOLLY WOULD!

ould you maybe want to, like, hang out sometime? You know, like, outside of the office?"

I looked up and smiled at my coworker Emily.

"Sure. Just let me know when and where and I'll be there."

"When" was two weeks later, "where" was a dented Prius en route to Dollywood, and oh baby, was I ever there.

Turns out Emily, who previous to this trip was a basic stranger, shared a similar passion for road trips, Dolly Parton, and general self-sabotage. I noticed the same fuck-it glint in her eyes two weeks ago, when she stumbled out of HR looking like a kicked dog, wearing Zara's sales rack. I told her that I had that dress, too, but that it looked way better on her. She told me she was sure that wasn't true, before breaking out in tears and running to the bathroom. That was the extent of our interactions prior to the day we both impulsively left for our lunch breaks and never went back.

The job was shit, after all, and the joint we smoked with our mediocre turkey sandwiches was talking really loud. Life is short! What if we died in that office? What if we got electrocuted by the copy machine in a freak accident and the last image we saw before we died was of those soul-crushing corporate fluorescent lights?!

The weed was right. We had to run.

After devising a plan to get our shit together as soon as we came back, Emily and I loaded her banged-up Prius with loose clothes and fatty snacks and hit the road. Em had never been to Dollywood, but her grandma always talked about it and she had always wanted to go. We sang the songs "Islands in the Stream" and "Jolene" at the top of our lungs, and somewhere outside the

Smoky Mountains I told her why I worshipped Dolly. By the time we got to Tennessee, I knew Em better than I knew some of my closest friends. Road trips will do that to you.

We talked about everything and anything with that slow, lazy ease that the open road inevitably brings. Nobody could touch us, and we were neither here nor there. Our messy lives were momentarily behind us, and we had a destination and, for once, an actual goal. Emily, like me, was a grown woman who was still trying to figure out what she wanted to be when she grew up. She told me all about her father's control issues and her mother's pathological lies. About her ex-boyfriend and his aggressive board-game-playing habit. About how when she told HR about getting sexually harassed at our old office, HR replied, "You should be flattered. Take it as a compliment that he feels comfortable around you." We screamed FUCK YOU into the thick southern sky and laughed like little girls at things that definitely weren't funny. We flashed pastures of cows and shook our titties into the wind and adopted the phrase "Whatever! Dolly would!"

Our lives were equally messy, but we'd figure our shit out when we got back. I was good at letting things fall apart and then burying the evidence. All it ever takes is a well-ironed Zara dress, I tell you.

Almost 24 hours later, we eagerly arrived at Dollywood, shocked by the lack of traffic outside the theme park. When we pulled up to the visitor gates, a sign that looked like it was written by a drunk 4-year-old swung to and fro in the thick summer wind: "CLOSED FOR RENOVATIONS."

We said nothing for almost ten minutes, and then just turned the car around. Why didn't we check ahead online? Why didn't we do our research? Why were we in the middle of Tennessee with no jobs, no money, and no real future plans?

When we got back to the city, we made a new pact. Not to get our shit together like we had tried to a million times before. Not to get back on track just so we could tell Aunt Sally at Thanksgiving how well things were going. But to slow down and stop trying to put ourselves back together when we were clearly falling apart.

"Fuck it," they declared. "Let's just freeze our eggs and marry each other."

I mean, shit, if the Queen could close down for renovations with no warning, then what the hell?

So could we.

I saw Emily only twice after that trip. She moved back home to Seattle, and I moved into my little brother's studio apartment. Maybe we'll cross paths again one day when we're both ready to reopen.

Sometimes, friendships last a lifetime; other times, friendships last a weekend. But like Dolly always says, "Doesn't matter how hard you try to outrun it—if that's who you are, that's who you are. It'll show up once in a while."

(Or was that my drunk grandmother?)

Things You Should Never "Just Wing" but Always Inevitably Do

Young enough to still believe in strangers, old enough to stay away from their candy.

1. Speeches

2. Baking cookies

3. Moving in together

4. Job interviews

5. All interviews

6. Being an adult

7. Vacationing in a third-world country

8. Labor

9. Finding a cozy sushi place that's super cheap but also really fucking fresh

10. Moving across the country

11. Consummating an affair

12. Finding a gas station in the middle of East Texas

13. Your entire college experience

14. Ecstasy with a group of people you like but don't love

15. Russian massages

But the truth is,
I haven't felt all
right in a really
long time.

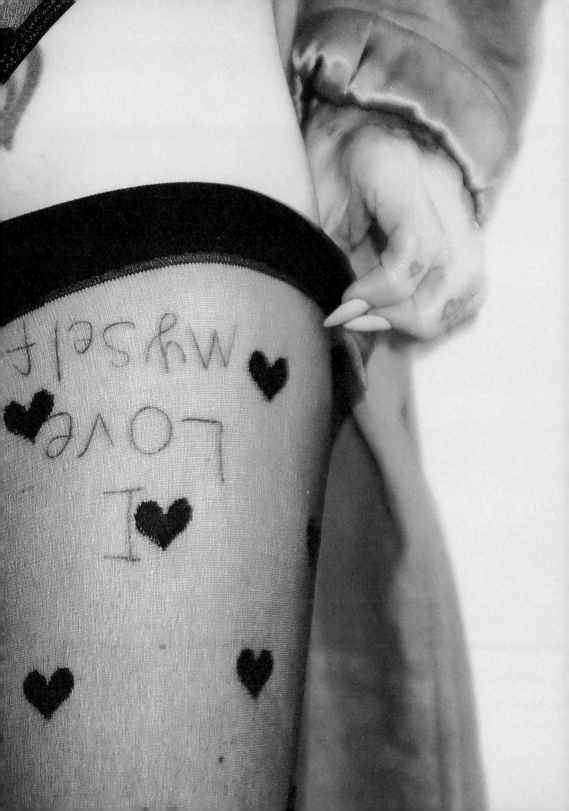

"24"

I don't always get stood up, but when I do, it's when I'm already in the midst of an emotional spiral.

7 a.m.—I am awake.

_____

8 a.m.—I am immortal.

_____

9 a.m.—I am confident.

_____

10 a.m.—I am searching.

_____

11 a.m.—I am hungry.

_____

12 p.m.—I am writing.

_____

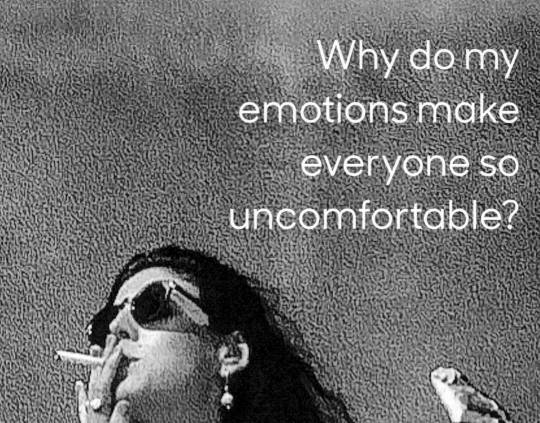

Why do my emotions make everyone so uncomfortable?

1 p.m.—I am planning.

_____

2 p.m.—I am questioning.

_____

3 p.m.—I am avoiding.

_____

4 p.m.—I am moving.

_____

5 p.m.—I am answering.

_____

6 p.m.—I am doubting.

_____

7 p.m.—I am hungry again.

_____

8 p.m.—I am thirsty.

_____

9 p.m.—I am smoking.

_____

10 p.m.—I am talking.

---

11 p.m.—I am impulsive.

---

12 a.m.—I am regretful.

---

1 a.m.—I am thinking.

---

2 a.m.—I am still thinking.

---

3 a.m.—I am missing.

---

4 a.m.—I am mortal.

---

5 a.m.—I am anxious.

---

6 a.m.—I am tired.

But I did care . . .

YUNG LUV

. . . because nobody loved harder than my sixteen-year-old self.

D o u want to go with me?"

I stared at the folded note and took the words in one by one to make sure I was reading them correctly. DO. U. WANT. TO. GO. WITH. ME? But before I even had a chance to process the words, I was already writing my response: "YES!!!!!!" In hindsight, I probably should have laid off the exclamation marks. But whatevs. I was 12 years old and CHRIS GREENLY wanted to GO WITH ME! *What a stupid term*, I thought, but that's what all the cool kids called it back then. I "went with" four boys in middle school. Chris, James, Dante, and Jack. With Chris we basically just ate lunch together and played basketball. With James we passed notes and held hands on field trips. With Dante we walked each other home and bought each other candy bars. With Jack we were best friends who also pretended to get into big fights about our "relationship" just to see what they felt like. We never had anything to really fight about, though, and at the end of most fights, we burst out in wild fits of laughter. We "went together" all of eighth grade. We went together to his dad's new apartment after his parents got divorced, we went together to my first funeral after my grandmother died, we went together to the movie theater, to the mall, to the store, to the creek . . . We went together anywhere and everywhere. Jack was my first kiss, and the summer before ninth grade, I bumped it up to second base and jacked Jack off. (Come on, I had to!) We stopped going with each other at the end of summer because Jack met another girl, at the pizza shop he was working at, and he just "wasn't feeling it anymore." Fair enough, Jacky boy, fair enough.

By high school the terminology changed. I didn't *go with* anybody.

Love is just a
requited crush
you've had a
million times
before.

I was the other woman, a position that I proudly kept for all four years. (And one after, if you want to count the time I almost pulled a Felicity and followed him to college.) His name was Jonny, and he was two years older than me. He was captain of the swim team and he smelled like CK One and chlorine. To this day I still get butterflies from the scent of overly antiseptic pools. I was obsessed with him my first day of high school, and by the end of the first semester he even knew my name. I drew maps through the hallways, tracking our classes so I could make sure I passed him multiple times throughout the day. Casually, of course. Until I rounded the corner and sprinted my bubbly ass to the opposite end of the school to avoid my fiftieth tardy. But the tardy-related detentions I endured were a small price to pay for that short moment of intoxication I may (or may not) have experienced when I felt the vibrations of Jonny's glance each and every day. He was dating a beautiful, smart, Ivy League college–bound junior named Dessa, and I was a desperate, too-tan, belly ring–wearing freshman with no thoughts of college beyond "maybe somewhere by the beach." I'm not totally sure when I started driving my mom's conversion van over to his house in the middle of the night to suck his dick, but it was wonderful. (Don't get me wrong, he fingered me, too. Or whatever you call it when teenage boys jam their finger in and out of you like a confused pubes-

You had me at "emotionally unavailable Australian with no job who's still completely in love with his ex."

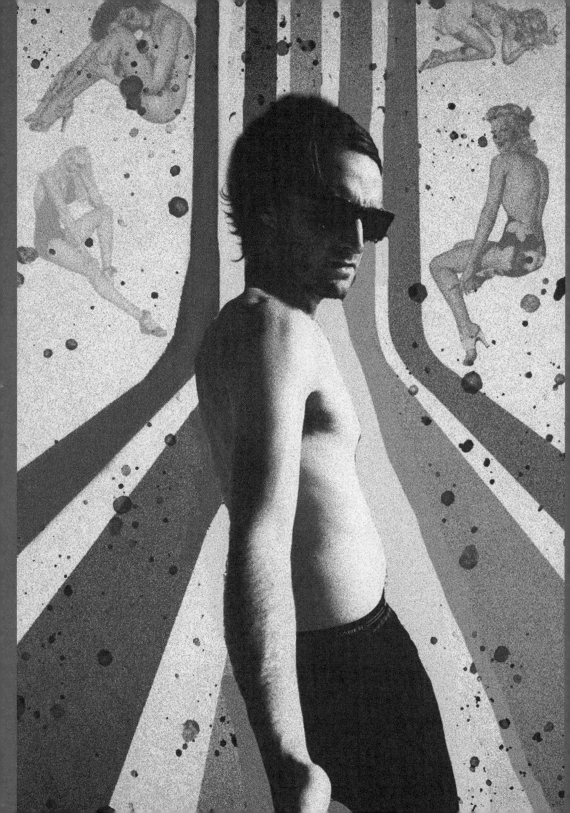

cent pogo stick.) We told each other we loved each other, but Jonny couldn't go public with our "relationship" yet. He needed to wait a few weeks. A few months. A few years...

The time passed like lightning or quicksand. Depending on our status. Where we stood. How close he was coming to leaving Dessa and professing his feelings for me. And I believed him. I believed him. I believed him...

At the end of senior year, I was left with about 100 pages of poetry, a file folder filled with saved AIM conversations, and one hell of a broken heart. What was I to him, after all? Was I the Glenn Close to his Michael Douglas? The Monica Lewinsky to his Bill Clinton? The one who got away? The one he "loved too much to admit"? It was all so confusing. He said over and over that I was "his girl," but was he ever "my boy"?

Post high school, I dated my first real man. All 21 years of him. He picked me up in his uncle's Oldsmobile and took me on actual physical, we-went-somewhere-and-enjoyed-something-together dates. I loved telling everyone I was "dating someone." It felt so mature. So solid. So legit. And yet, I didn't know why, but I felt completely disconnected from him. We couldn't enjoy each other unless we were experiencing some other form of pleasure. A movie. A meal. A concert. A bong. How could I have felt more connected to Jonny McFucknugget, who treated me like shit, than to Mr. Perfect, who picked me up and paraded me publicly? It was all very confusing. We dated for months and months. But he was never my boyfriend.

My first real boyfriend was next. And baby, oh baby, was I in love. Real, time-stops, colors-are-brighter, songs-sound-better l-o-v-e. I was 22 years old, and somehow calling each other boyfriend and girl-friend felt infantile and grown-up all at the same time. His name was Bobby, and he was so there, or so gone. He worked at night, and some-times I wouldn't see him for weeks. But that didn't matter, right? We had labels, goddamnit! Didn't that mean something? Of course it did.

Well, you know, until it didn't.

Bobby first started cheating on me a few months into our relation-ship. But only after I cheated on him.

We were both schmucks, but somehow the push/pull, make-up/break-up nature of our "relationship" kept things exciting. It was obses-sive and compulsive and addictive and dramatic. But loving someone should not feel like a bad habit. It should not be something that you impulsively pick at nor something you go out to get in the middle of the night because "I was so good all day!" It should not make you feel wonderful and then terrible. You should not shake and sweat without it.

"Girlfriend." "Wife." "Other woman." "Booty call." "Side girl." "Soul mate." The older I got, the more I realized Chris Greenly had the terminology right the first time. I didn't want to be somebody's secret. I didn't want to be somebody's drug. I didn't want to be somebody's prize. Hell, I didn't even care about being someone's girlfriend or even somebody's wife. At the end of the day, I just wanted a boy who wanted to "go with" me.

Anywhere. Everywhere. Somewhere. Nowhere.

But there.

Always fucking there.

HOW TO IGNORE YOUR LIFE AND TRIP THE LIGHT FANTASTIC

Jobless and single?

JUST DANCE.

Credit card maxed out and been eating most meals off a Star-bucks gift card your creepy uncle Tony got you last Christmas?

JUST DANCE.

Called off work sick and then saw Becky (fuck Beckys) from HR at the Chinese foot-massage place?

JUST DANCE.

Driving aimlessly through the city streets, contemplating the pros and cons of giving this dream your all or saying fuck it and working on a weed farm somewhere up north?

JUST DANCE.

In love with an emotionally withholding Australian who ignores your texts and no longer attends that yoga class you used to always see him at?

JUST DANCE.

Loving your big titties one second and then hating them for not fitting into cute shirts the next?

JUST DANCE.

Wondering when karma's finally gonna get ya for stealing that fancy candle from that expensive restaurant bathroom the other night?

JUST DANCE.

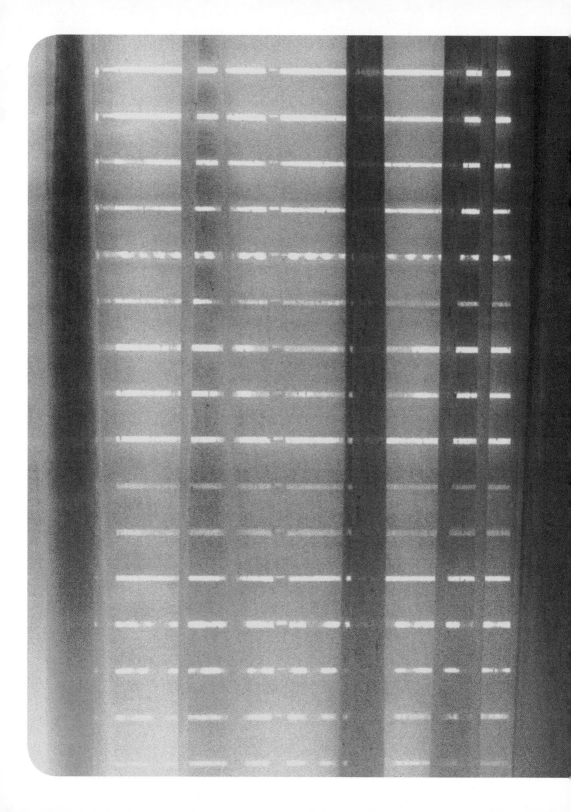

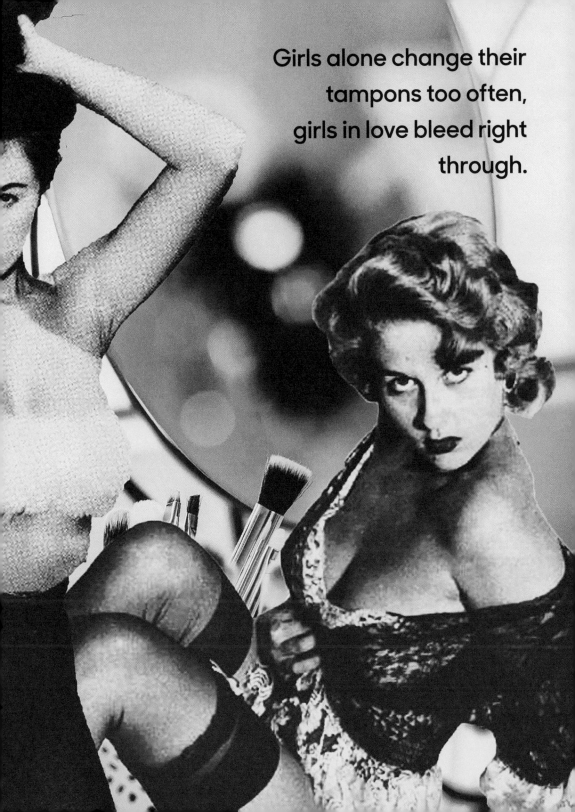

Girls alone change their tampons too often, girls in love bleed right through.

Choreography ruins dances, just like lines ruin paintings and readers ruin poetry.

A Very Short Story

(THE EX FILES)

order a cappuccino, you order an iced tea, we spend 45 minutes pretending not to want to fuck and/or kill each other. I ask how your sister is; you ask about my mom. Your hair looks different, but you still smell the same. We hug and it's so weird, our bodies pressing against each other for a little too long. I want to relapse. I'm never getting coffee with you ever again, because we used to be in love. The end.

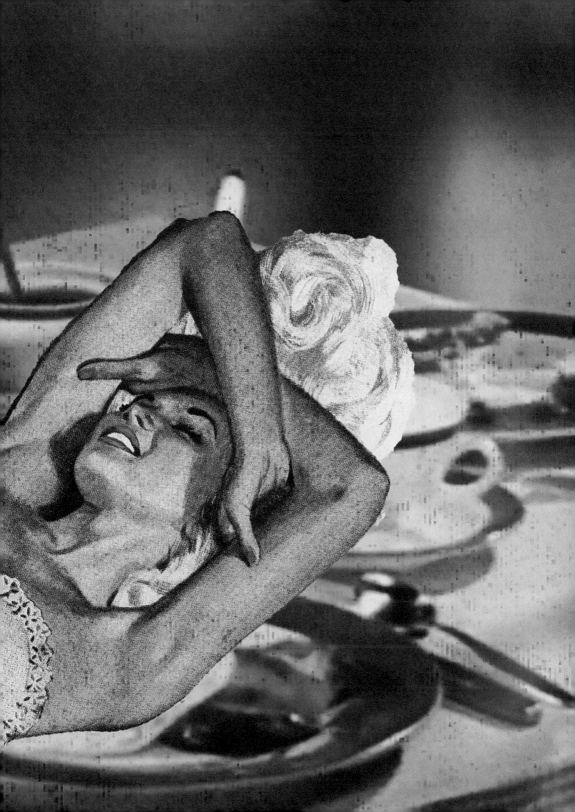

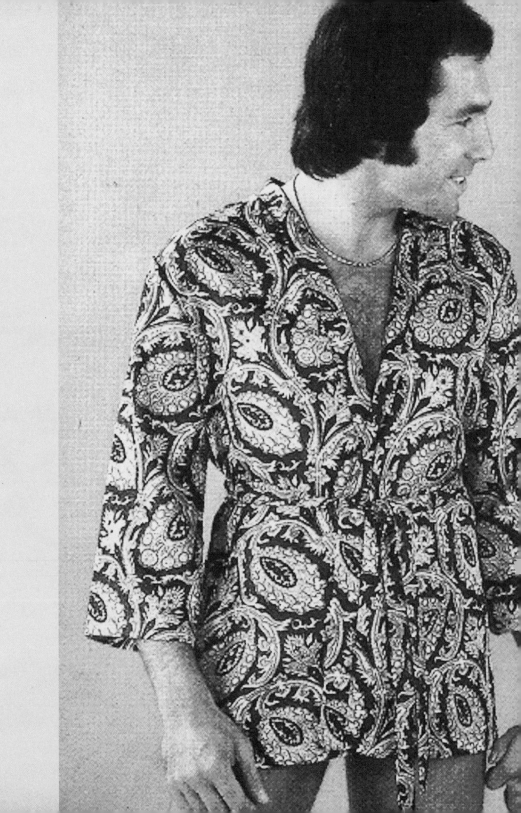

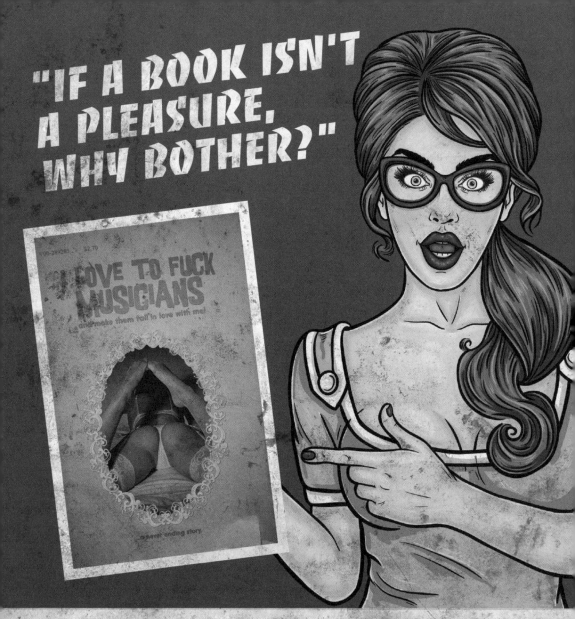

What did you want to be when you were a little girl?

SECURITY QUESTION SPIRAL

What did you become instead?

t's all fun and games until a forgotten password sends you on an emotional spiral that makes you question every decision you've ever made in your entire life.

Where did you go the first time you flew on a plane?

New York City. I was 11 years old. Other than an Astro van family road trip to Niagara Falls, I had never been out of the Midwest. And that trip to New York fucked me up. Not because of the stinky streets or the irate cabdrivers but because it showed me there was MORE. It was like my childhood shattered, because the world was suddenly bigger. I never woke up with the same naive bliss again after getting back from that trip. So yes, I blame New York for being a tease. I blame New York for ending an era. I blame New York for making me feel like maybe, *just maybe*, I would fit in better somewhere else. Better than where I was. Better than where I would have to be for the next seven years.

What is the name of the road you grew up on?

Conger Avenue. It was made of broken red bricks, and when we had rain, the entire street would flood. Kids from the neighborhood would flock to the nature-made river that had replaced our suburban street, and if you used your imagination hard enough, for a second it felt like you lived on the Venice canals. "CAR!" someone would yell as a car approached and tried to ford the flood. We'd scatter out of the boat-car's way and laugh as the frustrated driver was inevitably forced to reverse back to where the water was shallower. We'd splash and splash like fish in a contaminated lake for as long as we could, until the sky sealed back up and the road-river slowly got sucked down the clogged city drains. The older I got, the more I realized that water must have been disgusting, but no pH-balanced salt water–purified soaking tub has ever made my soul glow quite as good as that street-water cesspool from 1989.

What is the name of your first crush?

Benny Mendoza. Number 11. When I was in sixth grade our city spent every goddamn dime it had to build a Minor League Baseball stadium in an effort to revive our dying downtown. I had just gotten boobs and preferred to spend my time and money on Orange Juliuses and trips to the mall, so clearly I didn't give a fuck about some new snoozeball team. But everything changed when I won a contest naming the new mascot of the Akron Aeros. "Orbit!" was my submission, pre–gum franchise, mind you. And lo and behold, whoever was judging that contest (no really—like, who the fuck was judging that contest?) chose me, and I was awarded season tickets for seats right behind the dugout. Even cooler? I got to throw the first pitch of the VERY FIRST GAME ever played on that second-rate AstroTurf. I wasn't nervous—because again, who cared about baseball?—but my friend Ally accompanied me, along with my parents, so I threw that hard-ass laced snowball as fast as my skinny tan arm could. The crowd cheered, and as the announcer yelled, "LET'S PLAY BALL," I saw him. "Mendoza," his jersey read. I would proceed to become completely and utterly obsessed with Minor League Baseball for

SHOPPING ON PURE IMPULSE WITH WILD, FRIVOLOUS ABANDONMENT? THIS BOOK IS THE ONE FOR YOU.

Bleeding Through Supers
...and other things that happen at the worst possible times

Name _____

Street Address _____

City/State/Zip _____

the entirety of my middle school career thanks to Benny "The Crusher" Mendoza.

Ally and I rode the bus down to the stadium and used our season tickets every home game we could. We wore less and less as the summer got hotter, and we started collecting broken bats from our future husbands by hanging out at the dugout after the games. By August the lava lamps and Polly Pockets on my bedroom shelves were completely replaced by broken bats. A few of them were Mendoza's, but those slept next to me, underneath my bedside table. He started to pick up on my crush about midway through the season and began saving dirty balls for me. It would take me 20 more years to realize that shoving your dirty balls into my face doesn't mean you love me. Either way, Benny Mendoza was 26 years old and CLEARLY in love with me. Ally got bored with my bat-and-ball gathering and started leaving at the seventh-inning stretch. But I stayed the whole damn time. I was a REAL FAN. Benny was sweet and cool and tan and famous! Every day while hanging out by the dugout, I watched him sign at least ten autographs before I waved my wet n wild–painted hand at him. "Wassup you?" he'd always say. My heart melted into mush as I reached across the cage for whatever "collector's" item Mendoza could scrape up for me. One day late in the season, everything had been cleaned up and all Mendoza could find for me was a red Solo cup encrusted with chew. "I love it!" I said, as I threw it into my mini backpack and blew him a kiss goodbye.

When the season ended, I was devastated. Especially since Benny Mendoza left without saying goodbye after the last home game. I thought I'd never see him again (at least not until next year), so you can imagine my surprise when I saw him standing at the front of my third-period history class. "Hi, guys. I'm Mr. Mendoza. Mr. Saal's out with the flu today, so I'm your sub. He left this movie about the battle of—"

BENNY MENDOZA IS A SUB?! No, no! This is all wrong. I mean, I was happy to see him and all, but Benny Mendoza wasn't a lame middle school teacher, Benny Mendoza was THE CRUSHER! Benny Mendoza was an athlete. Benny Mendoza was a star!

"Hey. It's me," I said as I approached him after class let out. "Who?" He smiled. "Me. Broken-bat girl!" I'll never forget the blank look on his face as he tried to place me. "Oh, yeah. Wassup?" I forced a smile and shot the middle school shit with him for a minute or two and then decked it to the girls' room and locked the door and cried. I cried because I didn't realize Minor League Baseball players had to have real jobs, too. I cried because Benny Mendoza didn't remember who I was. I cried because Benny Mendoza didn't give me a broken bat this time, Benny Mendoza gave me a broken heart.

What is the name of your first pet?

Rosie. A kindhearted box turtle we used to draw on, who once laid eight rotten eggs. We let her go in the forest behind our house because we could no longer take care of her and "she'd be better off in nature." Two weeks later I found her crushed shell outside a sewer. Sometimes I still see Rosie and her rotten eggs in my dreams, but angel-Rosie promises she isn't still mad at me. I tell her I'm sorry, that I was trying to do the right thing, that I would have taken better care of her as an adult, and I'm sorry about her rotten children—that must have been so hard. She says she forgives me, and I say I believe her.

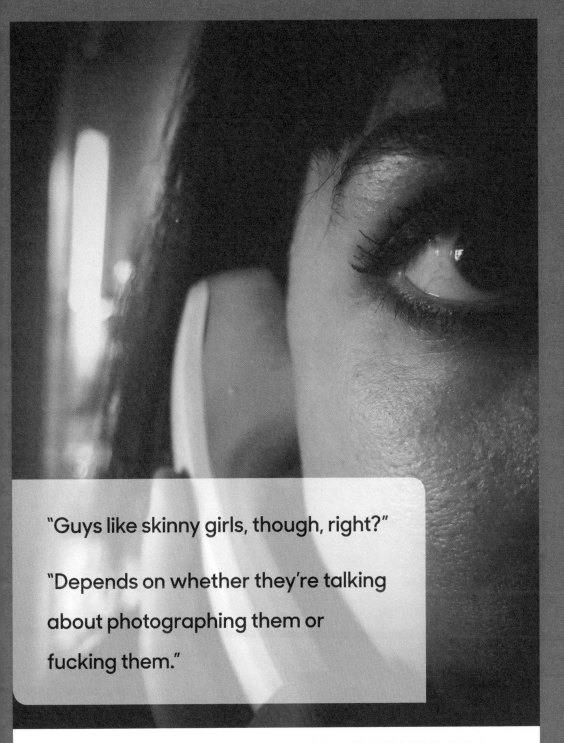

"Guys like skinny girls, though, right?"

"Depends on whether they're talking about photographing them or fucking them."

Crossword Puzzle

Across

3. That weird hour of night when it's too early to call off work and too late to text your ex.

6. His glasses! He can't see without his glasses!

7. You washed your hair with this in high school, when there were no worries or choices but Pantene Pro-V or this. Even though it makes your hair feel like wire, it still smells delicious, and sometimes when you're in CVS you sneak off and take a whiff and all your worries fade away...

10. Wear these all day because they're stretchy and comfy and make you feel like a real together type of gal, but NEVER, EVER do what they're intended to make you do.

12. The feeling starts in your body, right? The tingling, the loss of control, the rouge in the cheeks. Then, before you even know what's happening, it spreads — it spreads into your organs. Your heart beats rapidly; you can't eat. You have to piss all the time 'cause you feel so full of something, but you don't know what it is. Your fingers start to feel the air. It's thicker. The blues are brighter, and everything is suddenly on your side. A light sweat peaks on your face, causing you to glow, but you're not physically hot, you're just so alive that your body doesn't know what to do with itself. You smile, it's almost over, but in that moment, in those fleeting few weeks or so, curled up with the warmth of your severe emotional fever, rocking out to the sound of your own heartbeat... life suddenly makes sense.

14. Guys think this is their position and we just do it to make them happy, but actually we fucking love it, especially when they grab our hips / pull our hair.

16. Everybody is a little bit this. And if you don't think you are, well, that's when you REALLY are.

17. McDonald's has the best. Wendy's are meh. In-N-Out, go fuck yourself. Rhymes with "thick thighs."

18. Had flat feet. Not as hot as Barbie. You secretly identified with her more.

19. Strung Wendy along (and even made friends with her brothers, ugh!). Was always in love with Tinker Bell.

22. Cranberry juice is forever ruined because of this. Also, fuck you for breaking up with me and leaving me with no car, no explanation, and one of these.

23. Men-children from this continent (continent? country? surf resort?) will make you fall in love with them and then make it really hard for you to hate them when they completely fuck you over... because they're such... such lovers of life! (Alcohol, drugs, traveling.)

24. Most white girls are named this. This girl also probably kicked you out of the cool-girl group in middle school, accused you of being a witch, then hit you up on Facebook 15 years later, all "OMG, how have you beeeeeen???"

25. OMG, you can order it on Amazon Prime now?! Fuck yeah, you can. Gone are the days of filling up your basket with shit you don't need just so you can disguise it as "another casual item," while the judgmental cashier with the Jesus necklace stares at you like you just ate her firstborn.

Down

1. The boy WAS HERS.

2. They never have sales, but it doesn't matter, because there's something soothing about their nonaggressive approach. You have had multiple breakdowns in their changing rooms when you weren't even trying on clothes. You just needed to be alone. You always leave having spent at least 50 dollars more than planned. You love their dollar bins right by the door and still shop in their teen section, because the women's section seems sarcastically geriatric.

4. You got one when you were 17. Or 21. Or 36. Maybe you got more than one. It's okay, lady. It's okay. Your best friend held your hand in the waiting room and then drove you home and let you cry on her shoulder while she ordered pizza. You guys watched *Look Who's Talking* / *Raising Arizona* for comedic irony, and you cried some more but sort of let a few laughs out, too. You will love that friend who took care of you forever. Even if you've drifted apart.

5. Pentatonix won a Grammy for this one, with a living legend (hint: ivory skin, eyes of emerald green).

8. "Bastian! Say my name!!!" (The first fictional princess to make me feel bisexual. Later in life I dressed up like her for three Halloweens in a row, and once I met a Falkor at a party and we fucked.)

9. Model / unemployed is to female as _____ / unemployed is to male.

11. Her opening dance sequence in *Do The Right Thing* is the mental state I aspire to be in at most points in life. You are my queen and you are free as fuck. FIGHT THE POWER.

13. Don't ever tell me I look _____ after not seeing me for a while, because I will hands down assume you're simply saying I look fatter.

15. These rats of the sea have no nutritional value whatsoever but taste amazing as you're eating them while sitting in a red leather booth with a dirty martini in one hand and your ex's hand in the other.

20. A cookout with your girlfriends where you burn your suffocating underwire.

21. If they ask you out to this, they're not trying to fuck you.

23. Put this fancy mayo on everything. Fries, burgers, sandwiches. PUT IT ON EVERYTHING.

DOING DRUGS WITH YOUR EX

Do I
him,
am I j
lone

. . . IS ALWAYS A GOOD IDEA. It's a chance to get back to that sparkle-puffed cream pocket place of love where you used to be, via a psychedelic one-lane highway. Full speed ahead on the road to nowhere! I mean, really, think about it. All the pent-up anger, the unsaid words, the lonely nights spent headfirst in some pad thai, playing your very first interactions over and over in your sodium-soaked head like reruns of your most favoritest canceled show . . . Fuck it. When life presents shortcuts, one must take them. After this "trip" down memory lane, you will come out of your chemically in-duced rendezvous either reunited and more in love than ever or ecstasy-puking in his disgusting parking garage, wondering what you ever saw in the goon in the first place. Either way, your feelings will have shifted hot or cold, and as we all know, hell hath no fury like a shower stuck on lukewarm.

. . . IS NEVER A GOOD IDEA. Ask yourself: Do you really still like him, or are you just lonely? Drugs should only act as an enhancer—never as filler. For when drugs become a filler with no solid ground to enhance (no love to exacerbate, no scenery to saturate), drugs become evil. Evil little trolls that rub up against your panties in just

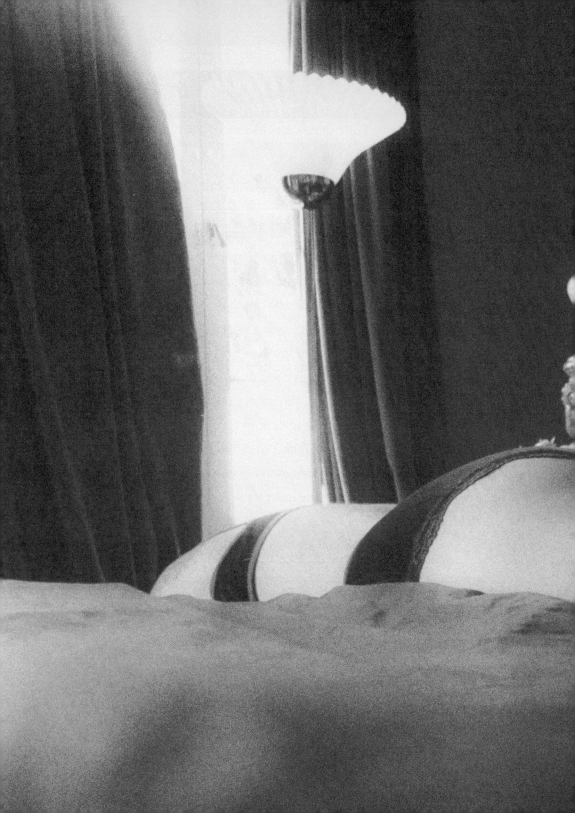

On a scale of 1 to calling your ex-boyfriend for a ride after getting kicked out of Trader Joe's for taking too many samples, how hopeless do you feel?

the right place and then disappear forever. If you scratch a nonexistent itch, it doesn't feel good; it just fucking hurts. No matter how much "fun" you and your past lover seem to have while under the influence of illegal substances, that fun will come with the depressing realization that you're living a dream underneath a beautiful filter that will inevitably be lifted, exposing the torn, undersaturated photograph below. You will feel great for two to eight hours, depending on your poison, and then you will wake up more confused than before, with a vague, unplaceable depression similar to that feeling you get after you eat a burger wrapped in lettuce.

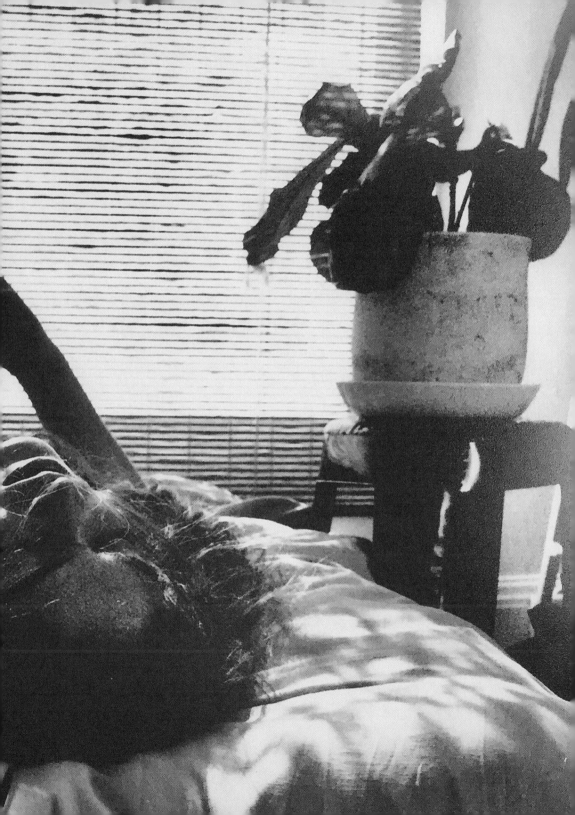

BAD PUSSY

A DARK ADVENTURE IN CAT-SITTING

feel guilty, though; we only went over and fed it twice."

"Fuck it. It's a cat. It's fine."

"But what if we get there and it's starving to death and Steve knows and he ends up hating us forever?"

The truth is, my childhood best friend, Jessica, and I could barely feed and take care of ourselves, so it was Steve's fault for trusting us with Ninja in the first place. Ninja was a nine-pound silver hairless cat that looked like an anorexic ballsack, and Steve was a six-foot-two blond ex-Mormon whose real name wasn't Steve. He changed his name to start his life over in L.A., and although I always had a baby crush on him (so mysterious!), there was something murky about the whole name-change thing that always kept me a few feet back. I met him at a restaurant we both worked at, until I got fired for eating from a customer's plate, and we remained close-but-not-that-close, so it was super weird when he asked me of all people to watch his hairless Sphynx cat. I told him I was allergic, but he assured me that he was, too. That's why he got a hairless pussy! No dander!

Fuck it, I said. Steve's house was nice and secluded in the Echo Park hills, and I could use his place as a refuge away from the 500-square-foot Hollywood shithole I was staying in with Jessica. We had tension over a lot right then—too close to begin with (our moms were literally pregnant together as neighbors in Akron, Ohio)—and so lately, I guess the only thing we could do was start drifting apart. We were too similar, and living together made us hate ourselves . . . and thus each other. We always wanted to fuck the same guys and wear the same clothes and discover the same music. One time in high school, we didn't talk for eight months because we got into a fight about who discovered *The Miseducation of Lauryn Hill*. Basically, we were always claiming one thing or another. Men, career paths, new snacks at Trader Joe's—we were REALLY bad at sharing. So when Steve invited us over for dinner to thank us for cat-sitting Ninja, we REALLY didn't know how to handle it.

Because the truth was, creepy as he could be, Steve had become a bone of contention for Jess and me lately. He was our most recent stake to be claimed. He was *The Miseducation of Lauryn Hill* of 2005, and both Jess AND I wanted to tell everyone that ONE of us had discovered him first. Quiet, mysterious, he flirted with us equally ("But I met him first!" "Not really! I visited you at work that night!"), he ignored us equally ("Have you heard from Steve?" "WTF, did he die?"), and he intrigued us equally. (He also starred in a few gay pornos and had a woodshed where he made coffee tables out of old rowboats.)

Six bratwursts and four bottles of pinot grigio later, Steve looked hotter than ever. And better yet? He had no idea that Jess and I had completely neglected both Ninja and his houseplants. Sure, Ninja looked a little skinny and the houseplants looked a little dull—but that was because they missed Daddy! Right? Right!

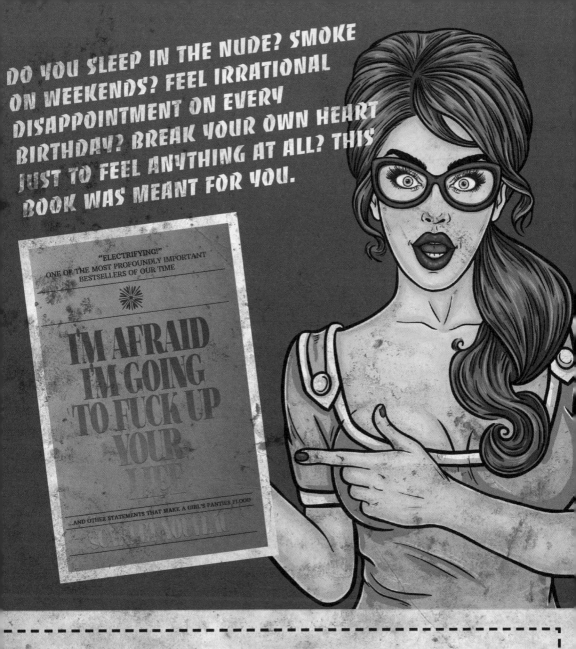

The more the merrier . . .

Anywho, cut to later that night—my eyes were blurry and I think we were talking about wanting to fuck Forrest Gump, when Steve told us he felt left out. See, that's the thing about childhood best friends: put some wine in us and all the bullshit disappears. The competition, the hurt feelings, the differently remembered history. Jess and I were untouchable when we got going. Our conversation moved so fast, outsiders didn't stand a chance. Sometimes we'd find ourselves speaking in weird nomadic cockney accents we developed as children. When we were in the zone, Jess and I were a symphony of inside jokes, fucked-up memories, and shared dreams. When we were in the zone, Jess and I were impenetrable.

"Psst! I can't see!" I whispered to Jess as I desperately searched for my missing contact. Had it fallen on my cheek? On the silk sheets covering the air bed in this weird-ass backyard tent? Had it fallen on Jess's ass?

"Here, put on your glasses!" Jess said, like Vada Sultenfuss to Thomas J. As she passed me my glasses, I quickly removed the other contact and flicked it on to the nylon tent wall like a dart.

"Are we really doing this?" Jess whispered, naked and thrilled.

"Fuck it," I casually replied. "Just don't eat my pussy."

I had thought about having a threesome before. Just not with my best friend. And not in a tent. And not while being watched by a judgmental hairless cat.

"He's coming! Shhh."

Jess and I huddled together and giggled like fourth graders hiding in a game of Sardines. When Steve arrived in his pajamas, we began to take them off.

"We don't have to . . ."

I put my finger over his lips and made out with him hard, as Jessica awkwardly rubbed my back. Steve was just trying to let us crash in his guesthouse (tent in the backyard) because we were too drunk to drive, but Jess and I had other plans. Because Jess and I had broken through that night. We were finally ready to grow up. After a quarter of a century, a hairless cat, and bucketsful of pinot grigio, Jess and I were *finally* ready to share.

RECIPE

BOOK

FOR GIRLS WITH HUNGRY HEARTS . . .

I've learned the best way to prevent your heart from being broken . . .

. . . is to act like you don't have one.

Food for the brokenhearted

Garlic Pesto Pizza with Cherry Tomatoes

Ingredients:

Dough (Store bought. Do not attempt to make dough yourself, or your 75 percent spiral will turn into a full-blown emotional tsunami.)

Pine nuts

2 cups fresh basil leaves, packed

½ cup grated Parmesan cheese

½ cup Not a Virgin olive oil

1 cup cherry tomatoes, chopped

6 cloves garlic, crushed

Directions:

1. Project your ex's face onto the store-bought dough and beat the living shit out of it. Form dough and set aside to rest as you make the fresh pesto.
2. Make pesto by combining the pine nuts, basil, Parmesan cheese, and olive oil in a blender and blend until smooth.
3. Spread a thin layer of pesto over the beaten pizza dough.
4. Top with cherry tomatoes and add lots of garlic, because the only thing you're going to be kissing tonight is the bottom of a chemical-laden Halo Top Creamery ice-cream container.
5. Bake for 13 minutes at 350°F.

6. Take out of the oven, prematurely dive into the only thing that's going to make you feel good right now, and burn the roof of your mouth.

Food for the newly in love

Twirled Spaghetti Carbonara

One of the perks of being in love, ah! You can at last make pasta without the fear of caving in to oblivion and eating the whole thing by midnight! You finally feel satisfied by a small portion of a fatty food. If only for a moment, you're eating like the fucking French! So go for the gluttonous dishes, including this creamy, fatty, not-nutrient-filled pasta that will satisfy you just enough, because your new lover is your second helping. And that love-juice has all the nutrients your body really needs.

Ingredients:

1 pound spaghetti

3 eggs

A shitload of grated Pecorino cheese

½ pound bacon or pancetta, cooked—but fuck it, just use bacon

Directions:

1. Heat pasta water. Fuck while water comes to a boil. Spill ingredients all over the floor. Sweep them up. Use what you can salvage as you continue.
2. Cook the spaghetti. Try for al dente, but then get distracted counting the freckles on your lover's back.
3. While the spaghetti cooks, make the sauce. Whisk the eggs, beat in the cheese, and set aside.
4. Strain the pasta, giving yourself a pasta-water steam facial as you pour it out, saving some of the water for thinning out the sauce.
5. Add the cooked bacon to the drained, overcooked spaghetti. Pour the sauce mixture over the pasta while it's still hot and toss to coat, adding the reserved water a little at a time until the sauce is smooth and creamy. Serve. Eat slowly, drink a lot, let your tummy be as nourished as your heart, and remember this moment of soul satisfaction, because this is literally what it means to truly be alive.

Food for the busy

Slow the Fuck Down Chicken Soup

I know you think you don't have time to cook, but the best thing busy girls can do is stop moving so fast and revel in something simple. Regarding consistently busy people, there is usually something missing. So this time, instead of filling that emotional hole with useless emails and never-ending to-do lists, fill that hole with SLOW THE FUCK DOWN CHICKEN SOUP! If you're lucky, while creating said soup, you might even have an emotional or career revelation that would have otherwise not come to you.

Ingredients:

3 medium carrots

2 stalks celery

½ onion

1 chicken breast

1 quart chicken stock

A lot of salt

A lot of pepper

Directions:

1. Chop the carrots and celery slowly, remembering forgotten moments from your childhood with each progressive carrot and celery stalk.
2. Chop the onion, remembering how good it feels to take a moment to cry.
3. Boil the chicken breast in the chicken stock for 20 minutes. Remove the chicken breast and tear slowly.
4. Add vegetables, torn-up chicken, salt, and pepper to the stock and simmer for 45 minutes. Sit on the floor of the kitchen and count your blessings, or if that's too hard, just count. To like 500. Breathe in and out. Ahhh . . .

Does running away burn calories?

Food for the lost

Rainbow Cereal with a Side of Kettle Chips and Hummus

You never know what you want to eat, just like you never knew what you wanted to be when you grew up. You prefer couch-surfing to subletting, and subletting to leasing, and leasing to owning. Nothing scares you more than routine or becoming a straight, monogamous, crispy-brussels-sprouts-eating bitch. Let your food match your peacocking spirit. This quick-to-please combination will surprise you and your guests but will also leave them hungry for something more substantial and subconsciously unsatisfied.

Ingredients:

1 cup Fruity Pebbles (dry, because milk smells like settling down)
½ cup crusty garlic hummus
5 servings Kettle chips (one small bag)

Directions:

1. Eat all items out of order, while watching or doing something else.
2. Trash the evidence of the meal, wake up, do yoga, go backpack through Europe, find yourself, then lose yourself again.

FEARS ONLY A WOMAN KNOWS

"Cover up!"

"Dress for success!"

Oh, you mean cover my boobs, wear something looser, and hide the fact that I'm a woman so people will take me seriously?

The size of my boobs does not determine my consent.

1. Trying on clothes in a fluorescent-lit fitting room in a store whose sizes run small. (After you ran into your ex-boyfriend's new hot girlfriend and then binge ate alone at Charley's Steakery.)

2. Going under anesthesia to get your wisdom teeth taken out by a 54-year-old man you met only 10 minutes ago.

3. Horseback riding with no bra and DDs.

4. Hiding Plan B underneath a basketful of unneeded items, only to get the cashier with the Jesus necklace.

5. Twelve-hour flight, foreign country, one tampon.

6. Accidentally releasing a small bit of air from your lady triangle in yoga class, only to unsuccessfully battle the breeze and have that brief opening turn into a full-out wind tunnel, so that by the end of the 90-minute kundalini class your vagina is straight-up breathing.

7.   Leaving for your lunch break and ending up in Italy.

8.   Getting pulled into an impulsive swim party without proper warn-
     ing and exposing your fur bikini.

I wish everything were as easy as staying in on a Friday night, drinking two bottles of lukewarm Chardonnay, sending 25 text messages, and spiraling out of control to the point of no return.

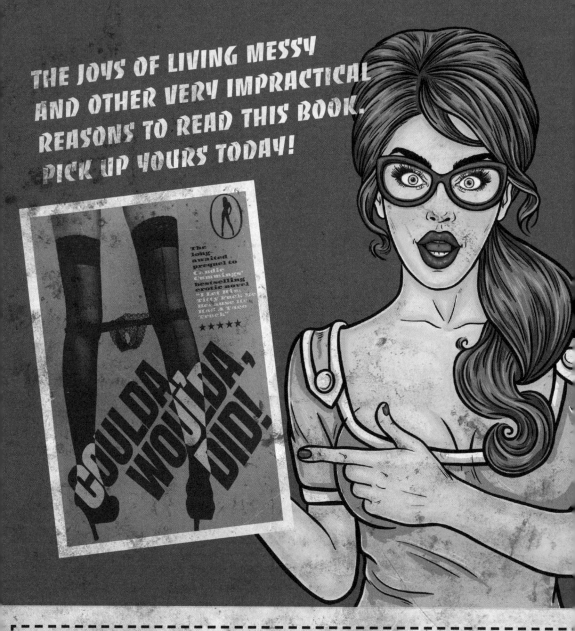

15 Reasons Why I Wore a Dress Like This

1. My little cousin Alyssa told me I looked pretty when I came down the stairs. Even though more than ten years had passed since the senior prom, and my cousin Alyssa wasn't a she now but a they, the look in their eyes felt similar to the way they looked at me when I came down the stairs all those years before. I looked like shit then (too tan, overly tweezed eyebrows, cheap chiffon dress), but in my cousin's eyes, I was a cool older-girl goddess who—if they had wanted to grow up to be a girl—they would have wanted to be just like.

2. I liked the blue color against my olive skin. I felt like a really pretty, unpretentious big-city Jew.

3. The other dress I was thinking about wearing looked like a sari, and I was scared I would offend my high school friend Priya, who I hadn't seen in eight years but who, according to her Facebook, would banish my cultural-appropriating ass for so much as buying samosas from Trader Joe's.

4. It was flowy and swishy and patterned in the stomach area, where I have always been insecure.

5. It was 50 percent off, so I justified spending the 75 dollars I saved on buying fancy panties that I promptly stuck in my glove compartment for "just in case."

6. The Tuesday I went to buy the dress, I decided to fuck the rest of the workday, have a "me day," and go see a movie. I had to be

Shopping? She loves it. Especially in little offbeat places.

Her clothes? Anything goes. In a smashing size 7.

Her cigarette? Nothing short of Viceroy Longs. She won't settle for less.

Viceroy Longs give you all the taste, all the time.

at the theater in 20 minutes if I wanted to get to my showing in time, so I couldn't try on any more dresses. This one would have to do.

7. My high school crush was going to be at the event where I would be wearing said dress. Most of his memories of me probably involve me in some Hot Topic tube dress or crushed-velvet romper from Delia's. I thought this dress looked mature, and I wanted him to see that I had, in fact, somewhere between then and now, become a woman. That I was whole without him. That after eight years (four during high school and four after) my crush had *finally* gone away.

8. The last wedding I went to, I wore red and realized that wearing red to a wedding gets you seriously scrutinized and mean mugged. Like you're trying to take attention away from the bride or something. (I was on my period, actually, and feared bleeding through. But obviously wearing black wasn't an option, so I opted for red. Whoops.) Anywho, to avoid unwanted stares at this wedding, this time I opted for blue.

"I wore this sexy outfit with one thing in mind: to get sexually assaulted!" —no woman ever

9. My grandma Laurie, who had a stroke when I was 11 and lost feeling in the left side of her body, had to spend the last few years of her life in a nursing home that I frequently visited with my mother. When we cleaned out her house in preparation for the move, I remember stripping her blue flowered sheets from her bed and smelling them. I would miss this house, and I would miss this bed, and I would miss my old grammy. This dress reminded me of those sheets.

10. The dress was a size 4, when I was sure I was a size 6 or 8. It made me feel skinny. And I wouldn't even have to cut out the tag to hide the truth!

11. All the women from my childhood clique were invited to be bridesmaids at the wedding, minus me and one other girl who jumped ship and moved to New York the minute we turned 18. For a few years after I left, ye old clique still tried to include me. To keep me in the group. I think they thought I'd move back home after getting the "big-city life" out of my system. But I never did. To be truthful, I could have tried harder to stay in touch with them as the years went on. But every time I went back home, we had less and less to talk about, and I found myself pounding two-dollar Fireball shots to trick myself into thinking I still had an identity among these girls, for an hour or four. Either way, the past two years or so had been quite radio silent on both ends, and I wasn't invited to be a bridesmaid. I think the bride and the other girls I grew up with felt more guilty than I

did for being so fucking relieved. Being a bridesmaid gives me anxiety. It feels ancient and cliquey, and like performing with a girl band you know will eventually break up when Cindy finally goes to rehab and Susie decides to go solo. Anyway, long story long, my old friends, the girls I got my period with and went to homecoming with . . . were all wearing green dresses. A green army of perfectly tailored, moss-colored bridesmaid dresses. And so I decided blue would be emotionally correct. Not too far off, not pink or purple or something too opposite. But blue. Just one color next door on the color wheel. Like maybe I used to be green, but I drifted.

12. I remember seeing a photograph of myself at the last wedding I attended and thinking how bloody dead in the eyes I looked. I'm sure it had a lot to do with the alcoholic Australian I'd brought as my date, but I can't help thinking a little bit of it had to do with the fact that I hadn't felt pretty. Inside or out. That I'd thrown on some wrinkled dress I'd owned for five years and hadn't been able to find any of the right jewelry. That my soul had sort of felt the same way. Disregarded and poorly attended to. Anyway, this time would be different! My dress would be perfect, the man on my arm would be different, and my soul would be a little more fed.

13. I looked so put together in it. It looked like things were finally all right in my chaotic, rumor-swirled-about life. Like I had finally grown up and become okay with being an adult. This is not, how-

ever, and will never be, the case. But it is fun to play dress up and occasionally pretend.

14. My ex-boyfriend was bringing his pregnant girlfriend to the reception. She seemed like the type of girl who writes Christmas cards and maintains a steady weight, so I wanted to seem like a cool, confident, artsy ex who wasn't necessarily dressing for attention but who also knows how to enjoy life and indulge, because I LOVE MYSELF WITHOUT HIM. So I got this long dress, painted my nails black, and ravenously ate steak dipped in the aioli that was meant for the fries, while smiling across the table at the happy twosome.

15. Most fancy fabrics make me break out in hives. This fabric didn't. I now realize oh yeah, dumbass, that's because it was synthetic as fuck. I think it's funny that expensive things give me a rash. You can take the girl out of the trailer park, but you can't take the trailer park out of the girl!

16. ~~To get sexually harassed by one of my best friends' fathers. To grant him permission to drunkenly whisper into my ear that he's wanted to fuck me since I was in high school. To subtly send the message that I'm a slut, who, because of my God-given DDs, is totally open to the idea of fucking her childhood friend's married 50-year-old dad. To make sure that I would finish the night in tears, after finding out someone I had trusted since childhood was "getting hard just looking at me." To make me feel stupid and~~

embarrassed for feeling so safe and pretty and confident earlier in the night. To make me love my boobs and then hate them. To ensure that I would feel dirty and gross and cheap when I pushed him away and told him I didn't want shit to do with him as he sloppily whispered in my ear, "Oh yeah? Then why did you wear a dress like that?"

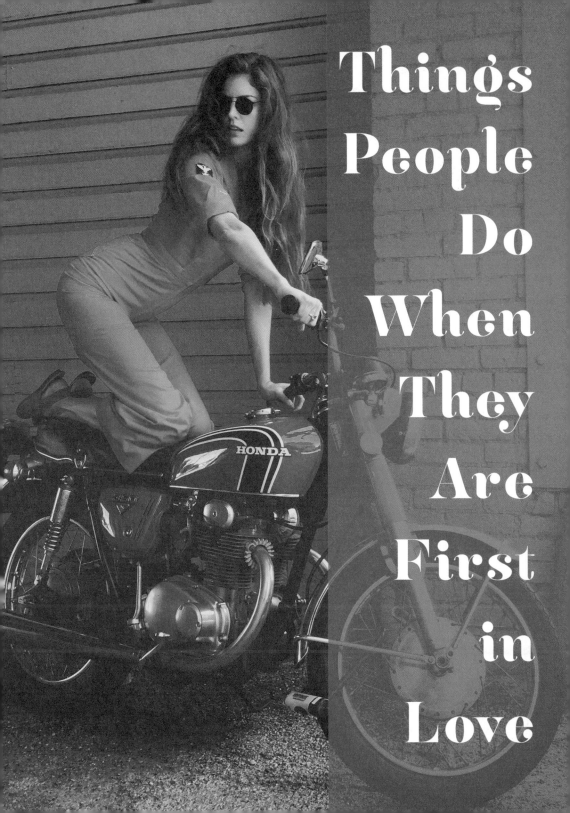

Things People Do When They Are First in Love

TOGETHERNESS
EATNIK • TWINKLE
R • WHY AMERICAN
CH WOMEN • THE
CLEAR TRACK TO
MEENY MINEY MOE
THE DERRIERE • ONE
SO HOW DO MINKS
TRICTLY PERSONAL

1. Go to Italy together.

2. Eat breakfast together.

3. Love each other's feet and ears.

4. Get chubby and don't care.

5. Wear fancy underwear.

6. Put on lotion.

7. Run away together.

8. Call "going to the grocery store" an adventure.

9. Flake on all their friends.

10. Fuck after lunch.

11. Watch each other sleep.

Ruby, Ruby, Ruby!

For gals who
break down, are
unreliable, and
occasionally
smoke

He looked so good in sunlight; he looked so good in taillights.

Whatisitaboutgirlsandcars?Thephallicgearstick?Thecomforting *tick-tick-tick* of the turn signal? The total control?

I always fancied myself a Prius girl. You know the type. Reliable RSVPers, socially conscious, always getting grilled chicken wraps and neutral manicures. All the women I ever met who drove a Prius had their lives together. They didn't let guys treat them like shit. They paid their parking tickets on time and got yearly checkups at the doctor's. They saved their money and made smart decisions for not only them-selves but also the world around them. When I finally saved (made 8,000 dollars, which I decided to immediately spend) enough to buy a new car, I knew it was time to grow up and get a Prius. If I got a Prius, I would become a real put-together type of gal, right?

WRONG!

But I didn't realize how wrong I was until Ruby.

I saw the beat-up old beauty on the side of the road on my way to the Toyota dealership, and suddenly the thought of getting a stupid soulless Prius made my skin itch. Who was I kidding? I wasn't one of those girls! I didn't want to be one of those girls! I was a tits-out, top-down type of gal, and this 1985 soft-top Mercedes was just the vehic-ular boyfriend I was looking for!

And boy, oh boy, was my baby beautiful. Ruby-red outside and brown leather inside. Sure, the paint was a little scratched and the cloth roof was a little torn, but these were just life's scars, you see! This car had a soul and a story, and it didn't matter that the air-conditioning didn't work or that it had more than 100,000 miles, because WE WERE IN LOVE.

I could save Ruby. And Ruby could save me.

All my friends tried to talk me out of it, of course. "It'll break down on you!" "It's a piece of shit!" "I'm not coming to pick you up when you forget to renew your AAA!" Everybody gave me every reason why I shouldn't buy the car, which, if you knew me, you would know only made me want it more.

I paid cash to the seller and didn't even bother having a mechanic look at it. I needed to snap it up fast before someone else bought it! And plus, whatever "issues" the car had would be fine. Who cares if it took premium gas and failed the smog check? You can't put a price on cruising down Sunset Boulevard listening to Tina Turner in your dream car, can you? Of course you can't! Freedom hath no worries!

The truth is, nobody could truly understand the love I had for Ruby. Not even me. Because unlike a reliable Prius or a cost-conscious lease, Ruby provided me with the one thing I couldn't love someone without— adrenaline.

Ruby was my Prince Charming. My Romeo. My knight in rusting armor.

Every time I entered that little tin can of freedom, our journey was an adventure. I was never truly sure if I'd make it where I was going on time, but time is no object when you're in love. Strangers loved to gawk at us and wave as we cruised by. Only a few radio stations ever worked, but somehow, they were always playing the best songs.

We couldn't go long distances together, but that didn't matter! I didn't *really* need to visit my brother in San Francisco, and plus, it wasn't my fault—my car just couldn't make it.

As time went on, Ruby started not being able to . . . make it to a lot of places with me.

It was gradual at first. No trips over 200 miles, no steep hills, no highways on hot days . . .

But the moment I'd get frustrated about Ruby's lack of commitment, the car would do something magical and sweep me off my feet yet again. A life-saving detour, an amazing song, a midnight cruise, a bittersweet conversation with a homeless man whose dad used to have the exact same car—the exact same car! Can you believe it?!

Life was wild and crazy, and the crappier the car got, the more money I threw into it. The more pictures I took of it. The more I thought I could change it.

Ruby loved me, after all! We'd been through so much together, good and bad and bad and good. Hell, the car even jammed its door when a guy it didn't like tried to get in. See? We had a connection, guys. A REAL CONNECTION! The kind of love you had to feel yourself to understand.

During my time with Ruby, I dated A LOT of dudes. Dudes who strangely made me feel the same way Ruby did, see: adrenalized, lustful, perpetually unsure of where we stood. Like Ruby, their attention was either *so* there or *so* gone. There was Derrick, the fashion designer, who had tattoos and scars and felt like he was from another era. Jared, the waiter, who played the best music and had the worst coke problem.

Like Ruby, they were charming, enigmatic men . . . with some huge red flags underneath the hood.

Then Ruby saved my life. Actually saved my life. After spinning out on the highway one night, we did two 360s across six lanes of traffic and, miraculously, I got out without a scratch. Ruby, however, wasn't so lucky.

My baby was completely totaled and had to be towed away to the junkyard.

Fucked up as it was, it was also heroic and romantic. Prince Charming saved my life! Again!

And then, while riding the bus six weeks later, it hit me like a ton of bricks:

I had let Ruby treat me like shit. I let *me* treat me like shit. I confused chaos with chemistry, and I guess it had just been easier to ignore the check-engine light than risk finding out what was *really* going on beneath the hood.

I had dated Rubys all my life, and I was done. I didn't want the cool guy anymore. I wanted the good guy.

It was time to grow up and grow out and get rid of the notion that stability means boredom and reliability means lame.

Six months later, I fell in love and leased a Prius.

Oh—and it doesn't count as saving your life if Prince Charming was the very thing that put you in danger in the first place.

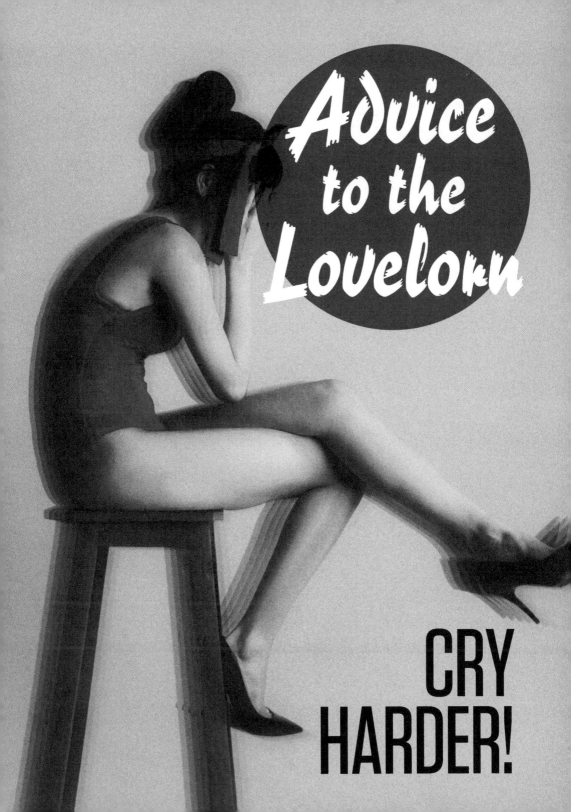

DEAR YELLOW-HAIRED GIRL:

There is this boy I've known for quite a while. Let's call him Tony. I think I am in love with him. The only problem is that I'm not sure he even knows I exist. We talk to each other sometimes, but it's only about reclaimed wooden desks. He sells them, and I bought three (over six months' time). I don't even need these desks, and I have put myself in debt just for an excuse to see him. I want to get a glass of wine and talk about anything BUT reclaimed wood, but I'm afraid he won't want to hang out with me in the REAL WORLD. What can I possibly do?

—A Nobody

DEAR A NOBODY:

Follow him on social media. Follow him in your car. Get to know his interests outside of wood. Get to know so much about him that you know the name of his crazy stepsister, who's always posting strange, semisexual comments on his Facebook page. Once you know him inside and out, casually run into him at his favorite juice spot while humming his favorite song. Serendipity! he will think. Once he is sure that you two are meant to be together, he will ask you to hang out. Proceed to date him for the next three months, until he finds out you hate Nine Inch Nails and that you accidentally friend-requested his uncle once. Return all of that dumb reclaimed wood, buy yourself

a sensual, overpriced massage, and move on to the next somebody.

—Yellow-Haired Girl

DEAR YELLOW-HAIRED GIRL:

I am a crier. I cry at least four times a week, and if I don't cry, there is usually something wrong with me. I have noticed that tears make everyone uncomfortable. They paint me as unstable, thin skinned, too intense, and weak. I used to pinch my thighs underneath the table in an effort to stop myself, but the tears didn't listen. Rarely do the tears come from actual sadness. More often the dam breaks in the presence of passion, frustration, or happiness. Why do tears get such a bad rep? Why is it wrong for your heart to sweat? For things to matter? Have we all just become too cool to care?

—A Cry Slut

DEAR CRY SLUT:

Do not apologize. Do not stop. Fuck 'em. Cry harder.

—Yellow-Haired Girl

DEAR YELLOW-HAIRED GIRL:

My boyfriend always tells me that I should smile more. What should I do?

—Frownie McFuckit

DEAR FROWNIE McFUCKIT:

If a guy tells you you should smile more, tell him he should be alive less. Dump him and move to Europe. Frown and vape and wear black and be happier than ever.

—Yellow-Haired Girl

DEAR YELLOW-HAIRED GIRL:

I've been dating my partner for about six months. At first, everything was candy and cigarettes. Sweet and deadly, morbid and alive! He asked if I wanted kids, and I asked him if he believed in God. We were deep and shallow all at the same time, and we spent every day fucking or cuddling or ordering pizza. Sometimes all three if it was a weekend. Anywho, lately there's been an energy shift. I can't explain it; I can only feel it. I looked in the dictionary, but just like the definition for "that feeling when you realize that your parents are no longer your heroes," there is no definition for this change in tone. What's happening in my relationship? Can you tell me more about this unknown phenomenon?

—Energetically Confused

DEAR ENERGETICALLY CONFUSED:

The moment you are describing in said relationship is commonly referred to as THE TIPPING POINT. Often occurring around the six-month mark, this feeling is disconcerting and all consuming. It's subtle at first: he gets annoyed when you try to tickle him and smell his neck in bed, he stops asking you to hop in the shower with him even though you're both in a hurry. You try to ignore it as long as you can, but you feel it in your heart and know it in your thighs… And then one day, homeboy's simply gone. You cry and you starve and you binge and you scream. You're not scared you're becoming your mother; you're scared you're becoming your mother's friend. You know, the one who always came over for TV-dinner night with tear-swollen eyes and blamed it on guys? You itch your skin because your chemicals are off without him and nothing feels right and the walls are closing in. And then one day you wake up and the curse begins to fade. You feel a little freer and want to get a little stronger, so you eat more vegetables and drink more water and remember that you're proud to be your father's daughter. One day far away, you will run into him and he will be married to a girl named Heather, who sort of looks like you, and you will wish him happiness and smell your new lover's neck, which smells sort of like his, BUT BETTER.

—*Yellow-Haired Girl*

HER/HIM
HIM/HER

HER: Dump me and blame it on your passion for "the arts."

HIM: Okay!

HIM: Damn, baby. How are you still hungry?

HER: The fuck did you just say to me?

HER: I love how you ignore me for days and then expect me to just drop everything I'm doing and come over when you finally reach out.

HIM: And I just love how you drop everything you're doing and come over whenever I reach out!

HIM: Just so you know, I'm emotionally unavailable, physically unreliable, and still completely in love with my ex.

HER: Great, let's date!

Perhaps the only way she could fully recover was to become falsely infatuated with someone else.

He was either *so there* or *so gone.*

After my first date with Ryan, I didn't leave his house for six days. I was completely blurry eyed and absolutely, 200 percent in love. Some of the blurry-eyedness might have been due to the fact that I didn't have (or didn't bother to retrieve) contacts for those six days, but the other part of the blurry-eyedness was due to the fact that my heart literally couldn't see straight. For years I had been anxiously awaiting my turn. To meet The One. To be knocked off my feet. To have my whole world flipped upside down, fucked sideways, and turned inside out. One could call me an anxious romantic, I suppose. Hell, some days I would wake up with the jitters just thinking about it! And if anything smelled even slightly like love, I would sniff it. I would snort it. Even if the smell was fleeting . . . even if the smell was inconsistent . . . I wanted it and I wanted it all. But I suppose "better to have loved and _____ than never to have loved at all" is a dangerous rule to live by for a girl who will fill in the blank with absolutely anything . . .

In the case of Ryan, that blank was filled with "ruined your most prized memory of your father."

My father collected boxes, you see. Mystery boxes. Puzzle boxes. The kind that you have to tilt and turn 100 different ways to open. The kind you hide your valuables in. Your secrets. Your great-grandmother's necklace. Your diary. Your leftover cocaine.

Although my father and I had a strained relationship, the older I got, the more we started communicating. Through boxes. Every time I maxed out my credit card and quit my job to join a friend on vacation, I'd find a local gift store and send my father a box. A burl wood box from Montana, a marble box from La Croix, an Elvis box from Nashville—it was my way of telling my father I loved him. Even though we were having hard times. Even though we were barely on speaking terms. The harder the box was to figure out, the more excited he got. Sometimes he'd email me from his AOL account (he still has AOL) weeks after I'd sent him a box and tell me all about the hours and hours it took, and how he finally cracked the case! He used lots of exclamation points in these emails about the boxes. My father never used exclamation points. He was a calm man of few words. But damn, did my dad love those boxes.

After getting home from the hospital (he was also a man of poor health), my father needed something to keep him busy. To keep his mind sharp and his spirits up, he decided to build me a box. BUILD ME ONE. I didn't know it at the time, but apparently it took him three months to finish. It was like building a maze, he said. He had to research, and saw and sand and glue.

And there, on my doorstep one morning, from the other side of the country, was a gift from my father. The box was open when I unwrapped it. (The boxes came "solved and open," and then you put them back together to lock them.) I marveled at the beautiful swirling burl wood and the craftsmanship of my father's hands. I smelled the box and I smelled his cigars. I smelled his piney cologne. I smelled his soul.

I took out the handwritten note that accompanied the box and started to do the millions of steps it took to lock and close the box.

But somewhere in between all this sappy father-daughter shit, my mind began to drift back to Ryan. I had gotten waxed on Friday, thinking that maybe he would text me and reach out this weekend. It had been two weeks since we'd had contact, and I was confused and wounded and hurt and obsessed. We were in-fucking-love a month ago. I slept at his house for a week! I skyped with his mother in Australia! We made blueberry pancakes for dinner and watched *Scarface*! So what the hell happened?

After our first date, he asked me to sleep over. He said he didn't want to fuck me (damn it!); he just wanted to sleep next to me. Well, sleep next to me he did. Until I fucked him. That's right! In the middle of the night, I rolled over and started touching him. I wanted all of him, and once I started he couldn't help it. We literally moved the earth that night and slept until 2 the next day. After lunch and walking his dog (it was like we were a real couple!), he asked me if I wanted to keep hanging out. My legs melted like Milk Duds on the asphalt below me, and I agreed. One more night turned into two, turned into three, four, five—we were completely fucked. I sabotaged my waitressing job and ignored all my friends and family. I sent out a few "I'm alive don't

You are my best friend because no matter how mad we are at each other, you will always be there to paint my right hand.

worry" texts, but inside I was completely dying. At least that's what it felt like. But not a bad death, it felt like a beautiful one. Like a death of worry and anxiety and pressure and future and past. Like a death to the outside world and anything other than me and Ryan. Like a death of caring about anything else at all. It was fucking FREEDOM.

During that week, we tickled each other's arms and listened to the Velvet Underground.

We grocery shopped and cooked lavish meals we could never finish, before we inevitably started fucking.

We showed each other baby pictures and not-so-secretly wondered if ours would look like us.

We watched whole seasons of cartoons from the '90s and danced naked on his roof.

We did mushrooms on the beach and ran into the ocean at dawn.

The day I finally went home, I literally felt like I had been hit by a bus. My life was now split into two parts. Before Ryan and after Ryan. When I opened my tiny apartment door, I collapsed onto the carpet and made movements that were something like a child making a snow angel. The ceiling was spinning. Colors were more saturated, and the smoggy air somehow smelled like honey. I couldn't tell anybody how I felt right away because I needed to take it all in. So I bought a pack of Capri Indigos (I don't even smoke) and drove halfway to Santa Barbara and back again, listening to some of the new songs Ryan had brought into my world.

I should have been arrested for Driving While in Love, because I'm sure I was swerving and speeding and slowing down at all the wrong times.

A few days passed and I heard nothing. Then, on Sunday, when I was just about ready to jump out of my second-floor window and probably unsuccessfully kill myself, my phone PINGED.

I lunged across the carpet from my bed and slowly turned my phone over with one eye closed. As if bracing myself for the results of a pregnancy test, I blurred my other eye and then slowly focused it.

IT WAS RYAN.

I let out a sigh so much bigger than the one from when I literally did take a pregnancy test and it was negative. Because somehow, in this moment, this result MEANT MORE.

He asked if I wanted to hang out tonight, and I appropriately texted him back two hours later. We had a blissful night, and then another one a couple of days later.

And then I texted him.

Nothing.

And texted him again.

Nothing.

And one more time.

Nothing. Nothing. Nothing.

My mind was in a scramble, and my heart was clinging to the railing before being flung over Niagara Falls. How could someone be so there, and then so gone? Did he go on a trip? Did he get back with his ex? Did he realize what a desperate human I was for quitting my job to stay with him? Was his phone broken? Was he not receiving texts? (No one is ever "not receiving texts.")

Nope. He was still here. In town. Chill and unaffected as ever.

At least that's what my friend Marissa said after she saw him in aisle 7 at Whole Foods.

SO WHAT THE FUCK?

I couldn't text him again. Not anymore. He'd clearly been ghosting me, and one more reach-out might take me into *Fatal Attraction* territory.

But I needed answers! What had I done? How did whatever we had break? How could he be calmly shopping at Whole Foods and not thinking about me obsessively, the way I was thinking about him?

I drank half a bottle of warm Chardonnay (because sometime during Ryan's and my "love affair," my refrigerator began leaking and then completely broke. But when you're in love that's how it works . . . you let shit break. None of that dumb real-life stuff seems to matter) and anxiously continued putting together my father's mystery box.

I was getting sweaty and impulsive and my fingers were itching for my phone, to say fuck it (again) and text Ryan.

AND THEN I HAD AN IDEA.

I grabbed a piece of paper, opened the list of contacts on my phone, quickly as shit wrote down Ryan's number on the paper, folded the paper, deleted Ryan's number and all our text history from my phone, and shoved the little piece of paper containing his number into the mystery box.

As I drank the other half of the bottle, I confidently finished putting together the box my father had built with his own two hands and coolly smiled when it was COMPLETELY LOCKED.

Moments later I smoked a Capri (by then I actually had started smoking—thanks, Ryan) and burned the paper containing the directions to unlock the box.

I've never had a lot of restraint, but now I had no choice. Now I would be the cool girl. Now I literally couldn't reach out to Ryan. Now he would miss me and come running back to me and I would have the upper hand!

NOW I WAS GOING OUT TO HAVE FUN AND SEE MY GIRLFRIENDS, WHO I'D ABANDONED DURING HURRICANE RYAN!!!!

After an underwhelming wild-but-weird night at an Irish bar called O'Brian's (for some reason Irish bars have always made me feel suicidal), I stumbled in a Johnnie Walker haze to a taco truck outside my stupid apartment. (Everything seemed stupid right then.) I ordered way too much, thought about that one time Ryan and I had made fish tacos and played Trouble, collapsed into my stupid bed, and shoveled a handful of cheese glop into my chops. I needed something to distract me. Something to fill the pit. The alcohol didn't work, the friends didn't work, and the nachos didn't seem to work, either.

Moments later I threw off all my stupid going-out clothes and put on one of Ryan's T-shirts. His pheromones attacked my nostrils and dripped down my nose like the finest cocaine there ever was. Drip, drip, drip. It was almost like he was next to me ... kissing me ... holding me ... loving me.

Next thing I knew, I was holding a hammer.

I had to do it. I couldn't open the fucking box no matter how hard I tried. I slammed it against my desk and even ripped out a drawer that I covered with a pillow and then jumped on trying to crush it.

I needed to text him. I needed to reach out. I remembered the first eight digits of his number but not the last two. And there wasn't any time.

With complete disregard for my father and my dignity, I lifted the hammer and smashed the mystery box to pieces. What used to be beautiful marbled wood was now emotional shards of desperation.

But there, in the middle of a pile of splinters, in what remained of my father's box ... was Ryan's phone number.

I coolly and calmly grabbed my phone and texted him: "Hey u ..."

The next morning, I woke up in what looked like a crack den. The stale, sticky nachos, the hammer, the torn-apart desk, the smashed-apart box ...

I was embarrassed and disgusted. But it was all going to be worth it. Right?

I grabbed my phone and flipped it over, covering my eyes. Ready for the best day of my life or the worst day ever.

I had ONE NEW MESSAGE.

It was from my father. "Hope you enjoyed the mystery box :-)"

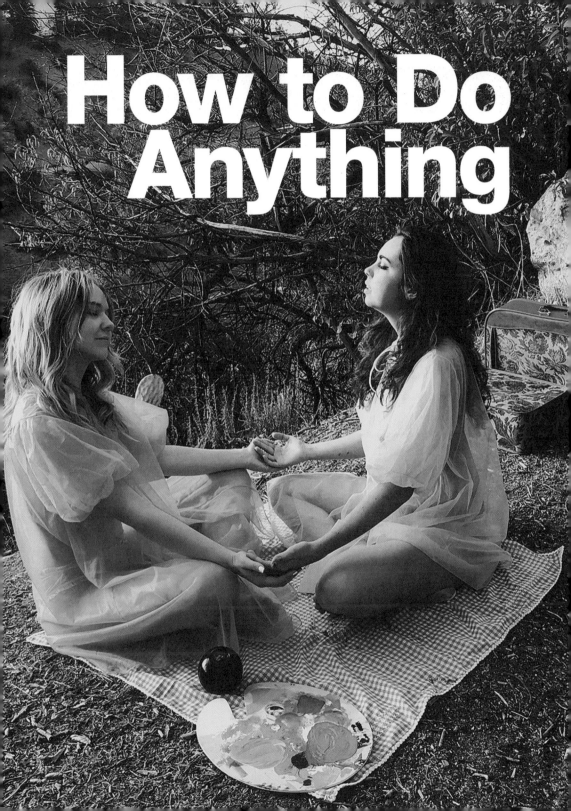

How to Do Anything

How to stop worrying about everything: Fall in love.

How to stop binge eating: Fall in love.

How to stop wondering what you were put on earth to do: Fall in love.

How to stop worrying about work too much, because nothing else matters more: Fall in love.

How to find something riveting to write about: Fall in love.

How to gain five pounds and feel more beautiful than ever: Fall in love.

How to stop overobsessing about your sometimes flaky friend who you love but who isn't there for you enough: Fall in love.

How to finally forgive your mother for all that shit she said last winter: Fall in love.

How to sing a great song even if your voice is terrible: Fall in love.

How to let go of grudges: Fall in love.

How to stop thinking that there can't be anything better than doing ecstasy alone on a Thursday night: Fall in love.

How to stop listening to podcasts and start listening to music: Fall in love.

How to wake up on the right side of the bed: Fall in love.

How to stop smoking: Fall in love.

How to start smoking: Fall in love.

How to finally understand why Thomas J. went headfirst into that bee-hive: Fall in love.

How to suddenly succeed at your career, because even though you're trying ten times less, your work is ten times better: Fall in love.

How to stop thinking, *That stuff only happens in books:* Fall in love.

How to fall in love: … ?

This story is a tragic one. Mad, rambling, and vagabond. All the good ones are, don't you agree?

The room was pitch-black, if I'm remembering correctly, until the string of a small light was pulled, illuminating the space in a clinical fluorescent haze. I squirmed underneath the white sheets, my stomach grumbling, my demeanor vacant, haunted, sick. Unable to sleep, I put on my furry pink slippers, buttoned my nightgown, and walked to the door of my assigned room, careful not to wake my roommate.

Quietly, carefully, I tiptoed along the dark hallway toward the common area and grabbed a piece of fruit. A harsh light turned on. I froze.

"What are you doing?" the warden snapped.

"I can't get to sleep. I don't think I had enough to eat at dinner."

"Just go back to bed," the warden ordered. "You'll forget you were even hungry in the first place."

Oh dear, I thought. *If only it were that easy.*

Early the next morning I rubbed my tired eyes and sat in a chair across from a nurse. The nurse checked my blood pressure, applying the arm wrap tightly. *Pump, pump, pump,* as my mind did its thing and drifted elsewhere.

Months ago, when I arrived, I was labeled suicidal and unstable. Addicted to and unable to handle love in a healthy manner. Severely susceptible to the fever. I didn't understand what measurements they could possibly be using when computing the chemical imbalance of unrequited love. They said I had the demeanor of a kicked dog. That I was as fragile as melting ice. They asked me if he ever hit me. He didn't. But anyone who's ever been in the thick of the fever knows that crimes of the heart can feel more violent than physical abuse, anyway. During my time here the staff of professionals has diligently tended to my emotional indigestion with a vast array of experimen-

Dirty Girls

*tal therapies. As if you could stitch together a broken heart. I was fed
healthy, nourishing foods to satisfy my insatiable appetite. Taught
coping mechanisms to express my feelings in a controlled manner.
Given two yellow pills a day to help me forget* him. *Why, my little
friends were guaranteed to numb it all.*

Hours later, after my blood pressure proved shockingly stable (I had
chugged beet juice the week previous and counted sheep during the
test), I folded my clothes in my room, with one barred window and two
twin beds. Frances, my roommate, sat on the other bed, holding two
manila envelopes close to her chest. Frances used to shoot love up her
arm five times a day. I liked Frances. She knew what it was like to want
more, more, more.

Anywho, it was an important day, because both Frances and I were
finally being discharged. And Frances stole our files.

Eagerly, I opened mine and stared down at the report. I knew what it
would say. That I liked the crazies. The daft ones. Scientists. Professors.
Drug addicts. Painters, poets, criminals, saviors. But this report had it all
wrong; it said they weren't the crazy ones—it said *I* was.

Apparently, I didn't attract the psychos. Apparently, I *was* the psycho.
Whatever.

Later that night, my taxi pulled up outside a large decrepit trailer in the armpit of the Midwest. The Ohio River Valley. I had been sent to live with a distant cousin of my mother's in a trailer park outside a town called Yorkville. As far away from my shadow as I could get, I suppose. Hate it as I tried, I couldn't help but feel like maybe the whole hospitalization thing was for the best. I felt strong and in control. Far from love and all its disastrous detours. Better than I had in years . . .

After paying for the cab, I stepped into the overgrown mobile-home community full of single-wide trailers. The color of the vegetation was undersaturated, the gardens overgrown. After a few tentative moments, I walked up a stone pathway toward the trailer-park office and passed a gorgeous brown-haired farm boy. He had the same husky voice and nicotine-stained skin as my father. I briefly thought about kissing him. After all, I had always had a little thing for my father. Most girls do.

As I continued staring unabashedly at the farm boy, my cheeks flushed with color, my hips began to slightly swell, a familiar euphoria pumping through my veins. Something horrible was happening. Something wonderful was happening!

I felt the slight beginnings of a peculiar fever. *And it spread like the goddamn plague.*

horoscopes

ARIES (MAR 21-APR 19) Has a loved one been giving you the cold shoulder lately? Been in one of their "moods" for far too long? Have you felt as if you're in a one-sided relationship? Have you been feeling alone? Is it because he broke up with you a few months ago? Are you in a delusional state of thinking he'll come running back to you once he "figures himself out"? WAKE UP AND SNORT THE ROSES, SILLY GIRL. Go get your hair cut. Short and shocking. Figure out a battle plan, because today JUST MIGHT be the day that you are able to break out of the delusion factory in which you're trapped. Your emotional hangover will slowly subside only if you begin to let it. The choice is yours.

TAURUS (APR 20-MAY 20) Reach out to your ex today! Cosmic conditions will serve your delusions well! He won't text you right back, but fear not! You can call him to tell him that you texted. Didn't pick up? Call him again! Go to his house with a bottle of wine! The world is yours! Don't cry because it's over! Cry because "it's over" *never* means it's over!

GEMINI (MAY 21-JUN 20) Mercury lurks in your 12th House of Privacy, while curious Saturn sanctions your urge to snoop. (You were right. He did fuck that girl.)

CANCER (JUN 21-JUL 22) If the one you're dating has suddenly gone cold, you may feel quite frustrated by the whole situation today, es-

Because every relationship is a long-distance relationship ...

Between heaven and hell.

pecially with the histrionic Leo moon throwing a tantrum in your 7th House of Companions. Purge your urge to go apeshit and end the relationship by creating a reflective interpretive dance instead. Later, when your beau is home from work and relaxing with a glass of wine, turn the volume up loud, turn the lights down low, and put on your one-woman show. If he is still cold after your performance from the heart, you may then go apeshit and end the relationship.

LEO (JUL 23-AUG 22) Lucky you! The lively Leo moon will guide you to meet your soul mate today. And they won't text you the fuck back.

VIRGO (AUG 23-SEP 22) Have you been feeling introspective as of late? Coming to realizations about your magnetic vagina being a tractor beam for lost souls? Suddenly looking back and discovering that lunatics with good hair seem to be drawn to you more than others? This emotional autopsy report makes total sense, since the 8th House of Honesty is circling the Jupiter moon. Listen closely and you may receive an aha moment from above that sounds something like this: "Maybe you don't attract the psychos. Maybe you *are* the psycho."

LIBRA (SEP 23-OCT 22) Steadfast Saturn creates a harmonious sexual connection to Mercury in your 6th House of Habits. What does this mean, you ask? It means today is a good day to throw your troubles in

the compost pile and take life by the titties. Eat that burger, fuck that boy, get that massage. Then turn this "me day" into a "me year."

SCORPIO (OCT 23–NOV 21) Your 8th moon is pulling you to revive a flamed-out relationship from the past. Enjoy, but be careful. It's all fun and games until you're a single mother with a baby named after the restaurant where you and your ex re-met. (OMG, Applebee is soooooo cute!)

SAGITTARIUS (NOV 22–DEC 21) Have your sensitivities been at an all-time high this lunar cycle? Have little things like trips to the grocery store ended in you having an existential crisis in the employees-only bathroom? Have you been thinking about God and the afterlife and soul mates and spiders? Has your current lover threatened to leave you over your increased capacity to expel extraneous emotion? Have you tried to talk about the laundry-dryer-ful of feelings in your brain but he turns on football instead? Listen to your friends and run far, far away from him, dear vibrating child. And relax! I mean, sure, you might have an anxiety disorder, but he's a closed-off, beer-guzzling man-child with three roommates, and they don't make pills for fuckboys.

CAPRICORN (DEC 22-JAN 19) The emotional landscape of your love life may be rocky terrain to travel today, causing you to nose-dive into the glory days of your youth, when liking a boy meant you threw rocks at his window and flaking was hard because texting didn't exist. You long for the days of *69 and physically talking on the phone, but you also know your ass hasn't picked up an incoming call since 2015. Nostalgia can be a bitch, and everything looks better in the rearview, especially when manipulative Mars is circling your frontal orb. But today is the day you must decide to fuck the past. And fuck it hard.

AQUARIUS (JAN 20-FEB 18) Have you found yourself trying to fill your love-starved heart with a myriad of poisons and alternate stimulation as of late? Are you nose-diving into a sea of drugs, work, food, creation, or crime to distract yourself from the most legal and venomous addiction of all? Are you afraid you're addicted to love? Fear not, beautiful soul! This past year has been extra hard on you. You tasted that high

for the first time, and nobody expects a crackhead to stop hitting the pipe while in the thick of it. Never get sober, little lover. Just get smarter.

PISCES (FEB 19-MAR 20) Run. Run from this new lover now. Do you hear me? GET OUT. This new "thing" is nothing but yet another relationship that will inevitably leave you chain-smoking Camel Lights just to remember what it felt like the last time he kissed you. Next month will be better.

Crossword Puzzle Answer Key

Across

- 3. FOUR AM
- 6. THOMAS J
- 7. HERBAL ESSENCES
- 10. EXERCISE CLOTHES
- 12. FALLING IN LOVE
- 14. DOGGY STYLE
- 16. MENTALLY ILL
- 17. FRENCH FRIES
- 18. SKIPPER
- 19. PETER PAN
- 22. UTI
- 23. AUSTRALIA
- 24. BECKY
- 25. PLAN B

Down

- 1. MONICA
- 2. TARGET
- 4. ABORTION
- 5. JOLL…
- 9. PHOTO…
- 11. CLOSE…
- 13. HEALTHY
- 15. SHRIMP
- 23. AIOLI

Acknowledgments

Thank you to all the weirdo friends who creatively supported me, modeled for me, and/or helped make this book happen in a various plethora of strange and glorious ways: Afton Reid, Mia Luisa Saltis, Dave Mullen, Kate Danson, Eli Russell Linnetz, Victoria McGrath, Kellie Pokrifka, Kansas Bowling, Parker Love Bowling, Sky Ferreira, Jessica Whitaker, Travis Jackson, Nesta Cooper, Pete Van Aucker, Amy FitzHenry, Christine Daley, @overheardla, Elizabeth Gesas, Doug Wick, Lucy Wick, Charlie Morrison, Alfonso Gomez-Rejon, Jenn Yale, Bart Breve, Tiffany Anders, Joe Vogelsang, Annette Lamothe-Ramos, Paige Ferrari, Sarah Zelman, Aidan Pilgrim, Elizabeth Burch-Hudson, Lauryn Kahn. And an extra huge thanks to Meredeth Kast who told me this should be a book and I was like oh hell naw, and she was right.

To my dad, Brian, my brothers Jaron and Joe, and a special hell yeah to my Mummy, Susan, for convincing me that I could take this project on, and for helping me tirelessly and embracing such a strange child.

To my amazing team at William Morrow: Liate Stehlik, Cassie Jones, Jen Hart, Jeanie Lee, Andrea Molitor, William Ruoto, Mumtaz Mustafa, Yeon Kim, Susan Kosko, Andrew DiCecco, Lauren Lauzon, and Camille Collins.

Special thanks to Olivia de Recat for her amazing paper doll artwork.

To my editor Emma Brodie, who has made a dream I didn't even know I had become a reality, and who never spanked me (that hard) even though I was late on Every. Single. Deadline.

And to my agent Meg Thompson, thanks for believing in me before I believed in myself. I never thought I could make a book, and I still don't even really remember writing it—so thanks for making the process feel magical like that.

Credits

Grateful acknowledgment is made for permission to reprint the following images:

Courtesy of Envato Elements: 7, 111

Sourced from Unsplash: 10–11, 23, 28, 33, 41, 42, 48 (eye), 54 (woman), 60, 88, 134, 211, 222, 223, 262 (images), 280

Courtesy of Pexels: 34–35 (guy and girl), 122

Sourced from Pixabay: 31, 34–35 (raindrops), 40, 46, 48 (book), 50, 54 (fire and scissors), 71, 148, 158, 204, 262 (projector)

Sourced from StockSnap: 158

Paper dolls courtesy of Olivia de Recat.

About the Author

Leah Rachel lives in Laurel Canyon, California. She spends her days writing, fantasizing, and fucking up her relationships. She's written movies and television shows for Universal, Lionsgate, Amazon, and HBO. She is currently showrunning the Netflix series Chambers, starring Uma Thurman, which she created and wrote. In addition to all that name-dropping Hollywood fuckery, Leah's alter ego, @TheYellowHairedGirl, has become one of her most honest and fulfilling artistic expressions.

HarperCollins books may be purchased for educational, business, or sales promotional use. For information please email the Special Markets Department at SPsales@harpercollins.com.

FIRST EDITION

DESIGNED BY WILLIAM RUOTO

Beach party by Billion Photos / Shutterstock

Color abstract blurred backgrounds by goku4501 / Shutterstock

Old newspaper background by HERE / Shutterstock

Pop art girl by Vectorpocket / Shutterstock

Seamless animal print by Patel BK / Shutterstock

Venice beach pier at sunset by KalpanaBS / Shutterstock

Library of Congress Cataloging-in-Publication Data has been applied for.

ISBN 978-0-06-283807-0

19 20 21 22 23 **SC** 10 9 8 7 6 5 4 3 2 1